Cryptocurrency for Beginners 2021

Ultimate Guide
For Trading & Investing

Table of Contents

Introduction

Chapter 1: Understanding Cryptocurrency

   Cryptocurrency: The Core Definition

   Decentralization

Chapter 2: Understanding the Risks in Crypto

   Understanding and Reducing the Risks

   Common Mistakes to Avoid as an Investor

Chapter 3: Understanding Bitcoin

   History of Bitcoin

   Timeline of Bitcoin

   Advantages and Disadvantages of Bitcoin

   The Future of Bitcoin

Chapter 4: Understanding Altcoins: Ethereum, Dogecoin, and Litecoin

   Ethereum

   Dogecoin

   Litecoin

Chapter 5: Understanding Altcoin: Ripple, Stellar, and Neo

   Ripple

   Stellar

   Neo

Chapter 6: Understanding Altcoin: Tether, Binance, and Cardano

   Tether

   Binance

   Cardano

Chapter 7: Understanding Safety and Security

    Fake Websites

    Fake Mobile Apps

    Tweets and Social Media Updates

    Email Scammers

    Common Bitcoin Scams

    Beginner Mistakes to Avoid

    Do Not Anthropomorphize the Crypto Market

    Diversify

    Skills Trump Chance

    Avoid Peer Pressure

    There Are No Such Things as Oracles

    Panic Selling

    Exiting Too Late

    Jealousy

    Building Your Own Digital Vault

Chapter 8: Understanding Investment Strategies

    Paper Trading

    Investment Strategies for a Beginner

Chapter 9: Understanding Exchanges

    Centralized and Decentralized Exchanges

    Cryptocurrency Exchanges to Consider

    Other Top Exchanges to Consider

Conclusion

References

Introduction

Anyone knows that starting out with a brand new topic can be a frustrating journey, especially when the tutorials and information provided are all at a higher level than what you can understand. Cryptocurrency is a classic example of a popular investment route that no one can explain in a simplified way. So, for anyone who is starting out, it can be quite a headache-inducing endeavor.

This is why this book is so important for your journey. *Cryptocurrency for Beginners* is exactly that: for beginners. People who have just started out in crypto and need a simplified explanation in order to kick-start their journey. It is a foundational book to have you start investing, as well as understanding the cogwork that runs behind cryptocurrency itself: a practical and unbiased approach for anyone who is interested in crypto.

Each chapter contains critical information you need to know when starting out as an investor, such as: understanding cryptocurrency, steps to stay safe, tools you will need, and investments you can consider. It is explained in a way that is simplified and understandable. Keep in mind, cryptocurrency has an occasional complicated side to it, but the reality is there is just a lot of information you need to understand. At the end of the day, you may find that crypto is actually not as technical as you feared, and once you remove the jargon and replace it with relevant words and information, everything will slowly start to fall into place.

Cryptocurrency has taken the world by a storm, and even the most successful trader will admit there is still much to learn on this topic. Its futuristic software and ideals have sparked many debates over the years, but consider that you could very well be getting involved in the world's next currency. Therefore, it is best to learn as much about it as possible, alongside the reality that you can indeed earn money in vast amounts. This is, however, if you play your cards right and have a certain element of luck.

This leads to a disclaimer: This book is provided for educational purposes but by no means is an absolute guarantee of your success. Rather, you can consider this a guide to help improve your chances of success. Anyone who guarantees you results in cryptocurrency should be avoided at all costs, as they are likely to be a desperate salesperson or a scammer.

Again, the world of crypto is quite gray, and there are still many uncertainties. But over time you will learn some relevant strategies and information that will help increase your chances of success as a cryptocurrency investor.

Chapter 1: Understanding Cryptocurrency

It is time to look at the very basics of cryptocurrency (crypto), as the foundational knowledge will help you with the more complicated ideas, strategies, and information that you will need on this journey. Not understanding what cryptocurrency is, or its nature, is like walking into a maze with a blindfold hoping to find riches in the end.

The world of cryptocurrency is quite futuristic, with a blockchain design that was way ahead of the curve when it started, and is still potentially one of the greatest ledger technologies in the world. No wonder people want to take part in crypto, as many do believe this is the future.

Cryptocurrency: The Core Definition

Everyone knows what money is, and the currency you use depends on where you are in the world. For example, America uses dollars, the British use the pound sterling, South Korea uses Won, and so forth. These currencies are more or less regulated by their respective governments and are still among the most popular forms of spending money.

Cryptocurrency, however, is also a form of money, only it is a digital version. Furthermore, cryptocurrency is secured by a form of cryptography. This removes the ability for people to make counterfeit versions or even try to double-spend (where people try to use the same coin on different transactions; this is only possible in the digital world). Most forms of crypto run on decentralized networks and are particularly based on a technology known as the *blockchain*. All these elements will be broken down and explained.

Blockchain

In order to understand the essence and foundation of most crypto, you need to understand blockchain. Blockchain is likely to be the most complex part of the entire system of cryptocurrency. However, it is important for an investor to know how it works. A basic understanding will allow you to work with it, as well as understand the advantages that come alongside it. Without blockchain, the popularity of cryptocurrencies would not really exist, and crypto itself might have just been a piece of fiction found in Sci-Fi movies.

Blockchain resolves a primary problem that has been holding back the idea of digitized money. This was the issue of 1) hackers and cybercrime, as well as 2) attempts to double spend. Now, digging a little deeper, blockchain runs on *hashing* technology, and in order to fully understand blockchain, a person needs to know what hashing is. It might seem bizarre how deep you have to break items down to understand them, but it will all make sense in the end.

Hash is a function that is used to convert a specific value (or information) into another. Hashing works well in cryptography because it acts as a mask over the information that is being transferred from one place to the next. The hashing blockchain allows a certain amount of data of any size to be converted into data of a very specific size. This is explained as: a changeable amount of input is converted into a fixed number of output. For example, this code: hfiwbrotiwytn456nbeoin4jonejownbopt is then placed into the hash and it converts to the standard amount of 7 digits: dkwu73n. But then, you place a new code:123, and it would convert it into 7 digits again: hw23or8.

What you should know, however, is that if you change the input number by even one character, the output code will dramatically change. This is a very important factor in blockchain technology.

Blockchain technology works as a digital ledger. It is a public yet anonymous display of transactions that occur online. The reason why blockchain works so well is not that it is unhackable, but its ability to detect change, fraud, and tampering is practically guaranteed. How does this work? Well to put it simply:

- You make a transaction.

- This transaction is run on the blockchain and processed.

- The information is changed into a hashing number and is stored in a 'block' of memory. Keep in mind, the hashing number works like a code, and any changes to the information on the block change the code.

- Now, someone else performs a transaction. The same process occurs, except the information is now stored in the second block, and the code from the previous block is stored in the second block as well. This is where it is linked like a chain (hence the name blockchain).

Therefore, if you change the information in block 1, the code of block 1 will change. If the second block's code of block 1 then does not match with block 1's new code, it will automatically change it back to the first block's original code (prior to the tampering). The same can be said for block 3, which now has block 2's code, and so forth. Now, a person could reason that if you change a block's information it will change the following block's code as well. However, here is the linchpin: there are several copies of the same code stored on other computers. So not only does the blockchain information need to match itself, but it also needs to match the copies of the same blockchain.

So in summary, if you were to hack and change the information on all the blocks of information, you would also have to hack into a certain number of computers with a copy of the blockchain. And finally, you would have a certain time limit as well.

This is the essence of blockchain. Decentralized blockchains are available to the public, so it is easy to see the transactions that are made. Yet, because of the hashing, the information remains completely anonymous. Having now dealt with blockchain, we will take a look at decentralized networks, and why decentralization is seen as such a huge advantage in the world of cryptocurrency.

Decentralization

Decentralization works in cryptocurrency as a system that is not regulated by one person or a small group of people. It does not have a singular point of authority, thus removing any control people may want to have over a particular system.

This brings a lot of security and anonymity to the table that many people crave in the world, as it solves one of the common problems known as *centralization*. This is where currencies or other items are operated by a single company, thus giving up a lot of control and security. The fact that banks have the ability to freeze or take away the control and ownership of anyone's assets is as daunting as it is a scary reality. Sometimes the freezing of assets can happen with good reason, but sometimes it doesn't. Furthermore, there is no guarantee of getting your money in emergency situations, such as stock market crashes and recessions. In essence, banks and centralized ownership are not reliable because of the ability to get corrupted or other issues. Furthermore, you always have to share your personal data, meaning you are naturally in higher danger of identity theft. A person's private information is meant to be exactly that, private. Yet how many times have people been contacted or emailed by unwanted marketing companies who should not have had access to their information?

With decentralized cryptocurrency, you do not have to share your personal data or any form of information that many if not all centralized platforms require. In fact, the average centralized platform tends to require your name, ID issued by the government, and many other personal pieces of information that expose you to dangers of censorship, identity theft, or more. When you work on a platform in which you are completely free from worries or stress about being monitored, it is understandable why decentralized cryptocurrency can be seen as so attractive.

However, there is a downside. Decentralized platforms struggle to be user-friendly, especially for people who are just starting out in crypto, so it takes some time and effort to learn how everything works. And because decentralized networks commonly remove the middleman, it works on a peer-to-peer exchange basis. Although this is quite often ideal, it does fail to be a very practical or easy solution to trading. This is because a peer-to-peer exchange normally works in an escrow account where the cryptocurrency or fiat is transferred off-exchange. This means that it is a multistep process that takes a lot of time and effort. Some of the projects and platforms are starting to adopt the automated process, but at this current point and time, many still have escrow accounts.

It basically means that easy-to-use trading is not one of the things decentralized platforms have managed, and it is surely something you will have to learn once you start trading more regularly with cryptocurrency.

Because decentralized networks can be quite a bit slower from time to time, it also means the liquidity of crypto is lower. This can certainly be a drawback for active traders and does increase the risk that is normally associated with crypto.

Cryptocurrency has a lot of elements surrounding it. Again, it is not as complicated as many people like to suggest, but there is certainly a lot you can learn. Keep in mind you should read and review whenever you feel a little overwhelmed. And be sure that you understand everything you need to successfully walk this investment journey.

Chapter 2: Understanding the Risks in Crypto

Cryptocurrency does have a reputation. Anyone who has done any research can tell you how it is filled with risks and issues. But truth be told, no system is perfect, and the higher the risk of investment, the greater opportunity for a higher reward as well.

Having a good grasp of the risk is an excellent way to navigate cryptocurrency in a safer way. Anyone who has trekked blindly in the jungle in search of a hidden treasure is far more likely to fail or get injured than those aware of the risks. Knowledge of the risks tells you where you can combat them and how you should mentally prepare. As much as crypto is a battle between logic and luck, it is also a mental battle, and understanding the risks plays a major role in how cryptocurrency can work for you. There are three key characteristics that are reflected as risks in cryptocurrency.

First, and this is the key defining factor of crypto, where it has established its reputation of being dangerous: it is *volatile*. A highly volatile market normally indicates sudden surprising changes can take place at any moment, any time for seemingly no reason. This can have a massive positive effect on a cryptocurrency investor, but it can also be a massive negative factor. This is why it is labeled as a disadvantage (but as an advanced trader, you could use the volatility to your advantage if you have the know-how): because of the major risk it brings to the table. It is not uncommon for the value of crypto to literally drop a couple of thousand dollars within the time span of a few weeks or possibly even a day.

Second, there is a lack of regulation that comes with crypto. This means that the government and central banks have no control over the crypto. This has appeared as a positive factor to those who have a distrust for banks and government because of the lack of control. However, a lot of its volatility comes into play because of this factor, and you have to keep this in mind.

Third, because cryptocurrency works in the online digital realm, it means it is an active target for both errors and hacking, which unfortunately can occur. There is absolutely no perfect way or code to beat technical errors or prevent hacking. Although blockchain is seen as an unhackable technology, many hackers focus on two other sources, such as the digital wallet or scamming people to send the money to them in the first place (through emails, calls, and other manipulation tactics). Most scams are quite easy to avoid with a little more thought and steps you can undertake to boost your safety.

Cryptocurrency can be impacted by forks (when the developers do happen to realize that fundamental changes are needed for the cryptocurrency to successfully continue) or discontinuation of trading. Cryptocurrency does carry extra risks, which means you have to do some extra work or research in order to ensure that the cryptocurrency you are working with is trading well. Although these risks are not completely avoidable, the risks can be reduced.

Cryptocurrency is still quite new, having originated from Bitcoin. This is an indicator that there is still a lot to learn from this platform. There are skeptics who say crypto may crash and burn, while others believe it could become a universal currency. However, due to its unpredictability, a lot will still need to change in order for crypto to even be considered as a legal tender on a global basis.

Understanding and Reducing the Risks

Although it is not entirely possible for you to remove all the risks, you can certainly focus on reducing them through various strategies.

The most obvious and logical tactic to reduce risks while working on crypto is to diversify. This is a common investor trick, used well beyond cryptocurrency investments. Protecting your assets by not placing all of them into a single digital basket is possibly one of the greatest ways to reduce losses if they do occur. However, it also depends on how much you can afford and how much time and energy you are willing to spend on them.

Another common tip to reduce the risks of any investment is through research, and with cryptocurrency, the more research the better. Knowledge is power, and extra time, work, and effort placed into finding out the necessary information can save you a lot of money. This is also important because you can deduce whether or not an investment is actually worth your time, as well as spotting scams and fraud that hide under the cover of good investments. So read the whitepaper (a document that has been released to investors, giving technical information about its concepts and plans) of the specific cryptocurrency of interest, and not merely what is written *about* it on social media (social media should never be used as a reliable source of information). Do not let laziness cost you a huge amount of money. Dedicate the time and effort to discovering what you need to know about the cryptocurrency of interest.

Double-check if you have the money. This means that you need to look through your financial books and understand whether or not you can actually afford to lose money. This is the number one rule for any investor anywhere, especially for those who have a high interest in cryptocurrency itself: do not invest money that you cannot afford to lose. You do not want to go into an investment in one condition and come out of it feeling a lot worse or in debt. Just don't do that to yourself. Investing is meant to help you grow your finances, not hurt them.

Keep an eye on your investment. This is not a place you can simply dump and leave the money unguarded. With crypto, you have to constantly monitor the direction it is heading. In order to be able to make a quick pull out due to a drop in prices, or whether the price is skyrocketing, you want to profit from this venture. But due to its volatility, any investor needs to keep a good watch on the direction in which their investment is headed. Simple as that.

Don't invest in a crypto asset just because everyone else is doing it. There is a mentality called FOMO, where everyone jumps into a trade in *Fear Of Missing Out*. This is where people are peer pressured into buying an investment that may not altogether be the most logical choice. Rather, make sure you are fully confident in your choice of investments. Only invest if you feel comfortable and if you want to, not because everyone else is telling you to. You are responsible for your own income after all, and therefore, the choice of where you want to invest lies solely on your shoulders. This reduces the risk of falling into traps and scams or outside pressure, and can certainly boost the odds of success when it comes to investing.

Common Mistakes to Avoid as an Investor

When you are starting with new investments, it is not uncommon to make mistakes, especially if you are new to the craft. However, it is actually best if you can avoid mistakes from the very beginning.

Here are some of the most common mistakes investors make that can actually be quite costly. It is best if you keep all of these tactics in mind, and avoid them as best as you can.

The first very big and common mistake is a lack of understanding of how technology works. Doing the research on cryptocurrency is important because it allows you to have an understanding of whether the goals of the cryptocurrency market align with yours. Yet, failure to do the research is one of the most common mistakes people make in the investment world. As absurd as it may seem, this is a trap people very easily fall into because they 'trust' the people advising them, without first making sure the other parties *are* trustworthy.

Overtrading is a mistake committed by people who start out in trading. Many beginners love to trade 20 times a day, but I can tell you right here and right now that this tactic is very dangerous. Many people lose fees or make losses for jumping blindly and hastily into a bad trade, which could have been avoided with a little more patience and perseverance. There is the harsh reality that 20 good trades just don't exist, and even if they do, the odds of you making or discovering the right ones are near impossible

Thinking of cryptocurrencies as shares is a third common mistake. Cryptocurrency does not normally work like stocks, nor do you have any form of ownership or claim to the company who designed them. So even if a company itself is doing well, it doesn't mean you will receive the benefits as an owner of the crypto. It is fully possible to have cryptocurrency's value sinking while the value of the company itself is rising.

Chasing cheap coins might seem like an appealing option, especially if you are on a tight budget, but this can cause a lot of problems and mistakes for you as well. Many people purchase cheap coins with hopes of receiving higher returns, forgetting to check the multiple factors that can get in the way, such as the real-world value and the volume of trading taking place with the coin at hand. Some coins are cheap just because they are bad, and they are not getting any returns in the long run.

Another common issue is leaving all the coins you have on your exchanges. You may be wondering what the issue is here, but the problem is if you don't have control of your keys, you do not have control of your coins. Leaving coins on exchanges for long periods of time exposes your coins to increased dangers of hacking and cybercrime. Your coins will certainly be more secure in your digital wallet, where you keep your keys stored as well. When you leave the coins you have on the exchange you are leaving the coins in the hands of the software's security instead of your own, which in and of itself should be quite daunting, considering exchanges are hotspots for hackers.

Not owning a hardware wallet when you are investing quite a bit of money into crypto is another mistake. What is a hardware wallet? These are wallets that are disconnected from the internet, meaning they are not always exposed to such a connection and are far more secure than wallets that are stored online. Hackers can only access such a wallet by physically stealing the device and knowing the password to access it. This makes safeguarding your crypto a lot easier than trying to fend off online hackers. Chapter 7 discusses wallets in more detail.

Falling for social media propaganda is also a common mistake. Social media is used to communicate and talk about practically anything and everything. And seeing negative/misleading headlines is not old news. However, headlines are often exaggerated for clickbait and can cause a flurry of panic or rushed decisions, especially when it comes to crypto. At the end of the day, social media is not a platform you should rely on except for picking up the occasional trends, nothing more.

A lack of understanding of the charts and fundamentals is something you should avoid. There are a lot of opportunities to learn how they work before placing a cent into investment. Charts and fundamental analyses are key ways of understanding the direction in which an investment is headed, as well as picking up patterns and developing strategies. If you lack the basic knowledge of these tools, then you are setting yourself up for failure. This is a common mistake you cannot afford to make.

Another common concept that many traders do not understand is market dynamics. Cryptocurrencies are all connected in their own way, and there exist more coins than Bitcoin (which is normally seen as the face of cryptocurrency). Make sure you have a proper understanding of how the market works, and this is best done by looking deep into the history of many of these coins, and how they are linked together.

Paying too much in commissions and fees is a costly mistake that can swallow up all your profits in one go. You need to be aware of the exchanges you work with and the trades you make. The costs can tally up, allowing you to pay excessively high fees, which may have been avoided had you made different decisions of whom to use. Especially if you do decide to use a broker, you need to be careful in your choice, as some charge excessively high fees. Do the necessary research on the prices of services before jumping in and consider the following: one charge may not seem like much, but multiply it by 10 and what do you get? Suddenly the fee seems a lot higher for a relatively small amount of transactions or commissions.

Working with the wrong advisor is another common mistake. You should work with a partner who has the same investment goals that you do, and make sure that you have similar training ideas, and that they perhaps have better experience than you (especially if you are a beginner). But don't follow anyone's advice blindly without double-checking and verifying the reasoning first.

In the end, there are still many mistakes which you can make. Consider getting yourself a tutor even to help guide you in the beginning and help you prevent any mistakes they may have made when they are younger. You are indeed setting yourself up for better success by focusing on learning from those around you who have a proven track record of success.

Chapter 3: Understanding Bitcoin

So, in order to gain a good grasp of cryptocurrency, what better way than to look at its history? And what better way to look at its history, than to look at the very first and original cryptocurrency. You probably know it: Bitcoin.

Bitcoin was the first cryptocurrency launched and run. It sparked a lot of controversy and debate, but is still one of the leading cryptocurrencies today and is highly unlikely to lose its first place anytime soon. It is important as a beginner to know the history of Bitcoin and its rise in popularity. Without Bitcoin, cryptocurrency would likely still be a digital dream.

History of Bitcoin

Bitcoin was registered in 2008 through a paper written under the name of Satoshi Nakamoto. Nakamoto implemented the source code and launched Bitcoin in 2009. However, Satoshi Nakamoto is probably a pseudonym, and no one really knows who the designer of Bitcoin actually is (although a lot of work has been done to try and discover their identity).

Bitcoin started the moment Nakamoto mined the first blockchain in January 2009. This was called the Genesis block, as it was the beginning of thousands more to come. And it has had its fair share of bumpy roads throughout the years.

Hal Finney was the first receiver of a Bitcoin transaction. He had downloaded the software on the day of its release. He was then awarded 10 Bitcoins from Nakamoto. Many analysts believe that Nakamoto had mined an approximation of 1 million Bitcoins before disappearing from the game. The alert key and control codes were passed onto Gavin Andreson, who became the lead developer in the Bitcoin Foundation. Andreson worked hard for decentralized control, and the path of Bitcoin started to grow at a rapid pace.

Timeline of Bitcoin

In the years 2011 to 2012, the first major users of Bitcoin were that of the black market. In February 2011, the value of Bitcoin started to rise by $0.30 per Bitcoin. However, on June, 8, 2011, it spiked to $31.50. The value dropped to $11.00 within the month. As you can see from the timeline that follows, the currency is very volatile, with currency prices swinging wildly.

- In the year 2012, it started at $5.27 per Bitcoin.
- In 2013, it started trading at $13.40
- April 2013, it shot up to $220
- Mid-April 2013, it dropped to $70
- October 2013, it traded at $123.20
- December 2013, it traded at $1,156.10-three days later dropped to $760.00
- January 2015, it traded at $315
- January 2017, it traded close to $1,000.00
- March 2017, it traded at $975.70
- December 2017, it traded at $20,089.00
- 2017 to 2019, Bitcoin's value dropped below $10,000
- June 2019, the price of Bitcoin reached above $10,000
- January 2020, it traded at $7,100.00
- November 2020, it traded at $18, 353.00
- As of 31 July 2021, it traded at $41,936.26

Advantages and Disadvantages of Bitcoin

(Icons8_team, 2018)

So,with it being the original cryptocurrency, you might naturally ask whether you should consider investing in Bitcoin? There is no clear black and white answer. You will have to see the advantages and disadvantages and assess for yourself whether or not it is worth the risk.

First of all, Bitcoin is the world's largest cryptocurrency at this point in time, and if Bitcoin were to fail, it could cripple the entirety of the cryptocurrency community. Whether or not you want to invest in Bitcoin entirely depends on your risk tolerance, as well as the objectives you have in mind,

The first advantage that is tagged to Bitcoin is that it is indeed a fast and very affordable service. Anyone knows the time and costs of sending money overseas can be staggeringly high, often discouraging people from even considering such payments. However, when you make the transfer via Bitcoin, the cost is absolutely minimal if at all existent, as the middleman is removed. Additionally, there is no limit as to where you can send Bitcoin. Considering it works within the digital realm, there are no rules in that specific manner. The world of internal payments and receiving payments are far less regulated.

Because Bitcoin is decentralized, it means that it doesn't have the regulations that exist with every legal tender that there is. It means it cannot be created by the government nor distributed by any means in the central bank. Decentralization removes the immense power fiat money (money that is regulated-legal tender, such as dollars, rupees, euros) tends to have over people, and there is no authority that can freeze, charge, or remove the coins from your ownership.

When it comes to Bitcoin itself, there are reduced risks of fraud at play, as well as higher levels of transparency. You can complete any transactions without having to give away any of your information to the seller, allowing you to remain anonymous. So the transparency allows you to freely work on the transactions at any time of day, while the anonymity allows your personal and private information to be protected from anyone who might try and exploit your information.

However, there is a flip side to this tale, where there is the risk of loss when it comes to Bitcoin. If any wallet files or hardware files crash and get corrupted, then you would have officially lost your Bitcoin. There is truly nothing that can be done to retrieve the information, and so the loss is very real. This means you have to be forever cautious of viruses as well, which can play the same role as a hardware crash and cause the loss of your money.

Economy and customer protection may also work as a hindrance towards Bitcoin. This is because there are likely to be a lot of hidden frameworks or loopholes in the design yet to be exploited. This means that Bitcoin is quite a risky choice, regardless of what you do to reduce the risk.

Furthermore, Bitcoin, just like any other form of cryptocurrency, is volatile and unpredictable in nature (as proved in the timeline, above). This means that despite any analyses and predictions made, there will always be a level of uncertainty. So keep in mind, if anyone tells you they can guarantee results in cryptocurrency, they are either a desperate and lying advertiser, or they are a scammer, because anyone with the proper and thorough knowledge and crypto will tell you that in this market, including Bitcoin, nothing is guaranteed.

The Future of Bitcoin

That may make you consider why people even try to predict the direction in which Bitcoin will go. Well, despite the level of unpredictability, people still try to forecast the weather. Forecasting occurs to be best prepared for what is to come, especially when people risk money in investing. It's only fair to get some idea of what could happen, and whether or not they should continue with a particular investment over a certain period of time. With Bitcoin, there are two opposite ideas of what people believe will happen. One sways to the negative, while the other sways to the positive. It is up to you to determine which one you think is more likely to occur and make your choices accordingly.

Ever since the COVID-19 pandemic, more people have been reverting to the digital form of money out of fear of recession and potential market crashes. This means that the popularity of cryptocurrency has been on a rapid rise, as more and more people accept and use it.

First, let's take a look at why people believe Bitcoin will fail, while others seem to think it will succeed in the decades to come. There is no real value when it comes to Bitcoin. The only value that exists is what people perceive it to be. This means the market can swing around like a crazed pendulum, where the volatility adds to the risk. It does not carry the same amount of confidence and certainty which a fiat contains.

Second, there is no force out there to stabilize Bitcoin. Fiat currencies have a government to back them up and defend it if push comes to shove (this does not mean that a legal tender will never fail, because they have before), but it does mean that if there is a force or pressure on a certain currency it has protection. Bitcoin does not have this, and in some countries, they have even made the use of Bitcoin and other cryptos illegal. Therefore, there is no huge power or power to back this cryptocurrency.

Third, Bitcoin is actually in competition with national currencies. A lot of people are claiming the value of Bitcoin, trying to have it replace the traditional monetary system. This is fatal for certain financial systems, meaning the government will then step in to eliminate the threat. This links it back to the reality that Bitcoin is not being backed up by a governmental system, but if Bitcoin poses too large of a threat to the country, it could just as easily be banned and left for scrap in the long term.

Finally, investing in Bitcoin is not the same as investing in blockchain technology itself, which is the driving point of value in cryptocurrency. Keep in mind, it is quite easy to separate the two, using the blockchain for other purposes, such as other forms of digital money or even anonymous voting. Blockchain is likely also to be used when fiat currency does end up becoming fully digital, thus kicking out the value Bitcoin has had from the start.

All these reasons are massive and overwhelming, making you believe in Bitcoin's destruction. Yet again, there is a flipside to this. Here are the reasons people believe that Bitcoin will never fail in the future.

First, there is a tight-knit community that has ensured Bitcoin's survival from the beginning. Even though Bitcoin had had its fair share of crashes and issues, it never seemed to drop to the point of no return. Bitcoin has always been able to make a comeback because of the community supporting it, alongside many technology developers working to advance the features of Bitcoin, and developers focusing on improving the design. All in all, there are a lot of people focused on Bitcoin's overall well-being, and this is a massive benefit: knowing people are looking out for this cryptocurrency, especially considering its value is based on the opinion of people, and not as a legal tender (fiat money). The community also tends to be active on social media, using telegram to communicate the latest updates, news, and information about Bitcoin.

Second, Bitcoin is for the most part transparent. This is always ideal for any group, making it very easy to see how Bitcoin is mined and how people can indeed evaluate a transaction. The new innovations that are created works as it should and the transactions of the blockchain's integrity are certainly confirmed.

Third, Bitcoin also passes the test of real-world usage. This is when people can use Bitcoin for a variety of reasons around the globe. Bitcoin is also used as a template for other cryptocurrencies, where the vast majority of crypto's original ideas start with Bitcoin itself. This means Bitcoin's design and the idea still remain one of the most popular ones to this day.

More and more people, as well as businesses, are accepting Bitcoin's nature, especially merchants. El Salvodor was the very first country to adopt Bitcon as a legal tender. This means more and more people are actually starting to trust the nature of Bitcoin despite the risk, and its popularity just keeps on growing. Bitcoin users can even use payment cards these days, and Bitcoin ATMs are even available for use. This shows the reality that some countries are actually accepting Bitcoin instead of fearing it, as some other countries do.

Fourth, With the emergence of new technologies, the use of Bitcoin is getting safer by the day. A reduction of risks is always a great advantage and very positive for the future. Bitcoin is becoming faster, the new technology that is getting developed makes it safer, and Bitcoin is following the path of internal development. Any business and currency that focus on improving are bound to have greater opportunities for success. All in all, it is striving to stay ahead of competition, and is likely to be one of the biggest reasons for its survival.

So which direction do you believe Bitcoin is headed? Do the disadvantages overshadow the benefits? Or do the benefits seem to crowd out the disadvantages? This is up to you to decide and keep in mind, Bitcoin is not the only crypto investment out there. It is only mentioned first because of the relevant role it has played in the overall growth and invention of cryptocurrency. But it is best to take a look at the others, and the advantages they bring to the table, before you make a decision about Bitcoin. All in all, Bitcoin is still running first in the game, but no one knows whether it will keep its position at the top of the mountain.

Chapter 4: Understanding Altcoins: Ethereum, Dogecoin, and Litecoin

So, you would like to invest in cryptocurrency, but have no idea what cryptocurrency you should consider, or even where to begin. It is good to take a look at some of the most successful cryptocurrencies so far, especially if you are a beginner. When starting out, it is best to build experience before tackling cryptocurrencies that are new and less known. Even so, it's risky to tackle crypto that few know about, and most professionals will go for what has indeed been tried and true. That does not eliminate all the risks that come with crypto but certainly can give you a better idea of which way to go.

Ethereum

(WorldSpectrum, 2018)

Ethereum is more than just a cryptocurrency. It is a blockchain-based platform that does have its own crypto, called Ether. It even has its very own programming language, called Solidity.

This cryptocurrency works as a public ledger, in which it both verifies as well as records transactions that take place. Ethereum happens to be in second place in the race of cryptocurrency and has been proven to be quite a resourceful software so far.

Ethereum was published in July 2015 by a group of people who were quite enthusiastic about blockchain. They designed it to work via *smart contracts*. This reduces fraud, downtime, or tampering. Smart contracts work like real-life contracts, with the reality that certain expectations need to be fulfilled and verified before the funding is released. It is an effective way of being able to create deals without necessarily having to trust anyone, as the program is unbiased and removes the bribable middleman who normally comes into play.

Ethereum is also known as a 'programmable blockchain,' which means people can see the platform as a marketplace for other apps, games, and financial services. They are normally paid for via tokens (Ether or ETH) and are quite safe from censorship, fraud, and other issues.

Ethereum was the first software using the blockchain design for more than cryptocurrency technology, but rather expanded a little beyond that. This unique approach was one of the major reasons it rose in popularity. However, it reached a sudden turn in 2016, when a hacker exploited a weakness and stole $50 million worth of Ether.

A lot of work and effort was put in to ensure a hack like this was not exploited again, and Ethereum had also faced a few critiques, such as how Ethereum's Ether tends to reflect similar prices to Bitcoin, causing much speculation. Each of these networks also demands a lot of energy and electricity, which in and of itself contributed to a lot of fossil fuel pollution.

Pros and Cons of Ethereum

Ether is a very complex form of crypto. This means, in ways of technology and structure, it is far more complex in comparison to Bitcoin. This might seem like an odd advantage, but in reality, it means it has more inherent value due to the services it can provide than merely the crypto itself. The provision of different services does make it more entrepreneurial.

Ether itself is also known to be more affordable, where a person can easily trade it for a couple of hundred dollars instead of thousands, which is currently the case for Bitcoin. And because it is second in the crypto market, its popularity adds another layer of security.

However, it is still highly volatile, meaning that the more you invest, the more you can earn, but the more you can lose as well, and drastically so. This is where the greater risk meets the greater loss or reward. But the loss is far more painful to experience and should be taken into consideration.

Due to its lower level of popularity in comparison with Bitcoin, this can lead to more liquidity issues, where finding a buyer may be more difficult in comparison to Bitcoin. This is always an aspect to take into consideration, as there are times you might want to buy or sell a cryptocurrency quickly (due to its volatile nature).

Dogecoin

(KNFind, 2021)

No one would have ever thought that the crypto which was founded as a joke would turn into such a profitable enterprise, but it did. Dogecoin is still thriving, and even more so under the recommendations of Elon Musk, one of the world's richest men.

Dogecoin is known to be a peer-to-peer cryptocurrency that is an open-source software. It is also, like Ethereum, an altcoin (coins that are not Bitcoin), and was designed to be a sarcastic meme coin. However, despite being created as a joke, it still has its advantages. It works on the same kind of technology that comes from Litecoin, and the main reason why it is popular is because of its affordable prices and unlimited supply.

In 2017, Dogecoin shot up in popularity and pricing, but the bubble burst, and Dogecoin lost a lot of the value it had originally worked for. But it had key supporters who remained and traded with it, keeping it very much alive and moving. Slowly but surely it started to climb in value, making it still one of the most prominent and popular cryptocurrency to this day.

Pros and Cons of Dogecoin

Day trading is a very good way to profit on this platform, using the volatility of the coin to your own advantage. If you like to have a more hands-on approach, then this is surely the coin to consider. However, it is best to learn day trading via simulations before actually practicing with legitimate money.

Dogecoin also has a large social media fandom, an odd advantage in comparison to many other cryptocurrencies. Dogecoins have fans spread all across social media, and you can easily use it to monitor the direction it is going with less concern of scamming or fraud (but still be extremely cautious when using social media as a source of information).

The irony remains that at this point and time, Elon Musk's recommendation revived many of the interests running rampant with Dogecoin. His recommendation of the coin itself sparked the interest of thousands of eager investors, and allowed Dogecoin's sudden rise in popularity.

DOGE (Dogecoin's currency) has a very friendly feel as they have started contributing to their fair share of social cases. Some of the Dogecoins were used to raise funds for the Jamaican Bobsled Team for the 2014 Winter Olympics in Russia. Dogecoin has also been used to sponsor other athletes, thus giving the appearance and reality that is giving back to the community.

Trade volumes on DOGE have also been on a rapid rise. This is always a positive sign, as it means the price and value of Dogecoin are on the rise. More exchanges have also been starting to list Dogecoin, making it easier to sell a variety of popular platforms, thus boosting its current liquidity. The future looks quite bright for this growing altcoin, as it even works at a faster speed than Bitcoin.

Dogecoin is also a community-based cryptocurrency, where people relate to and enjoy the crypto for being more than just a digital currency but also for the sarcastic meme from which it derived. Basically, there is a large amount of fan loyalty based on why it was created, and the fact is that Dogecoin remains popular on both crypto worlds and social media.

But, to take a peek at a different side, Dogecoin has questionable surroundings in regards to what the leadership believes regarding its place in cryptocurrency. Leaders are meant to be an example, but this is not the case for Dogecoin. The co-founder of Dogecoin had sold all of his Dogecoins in 2015, using the money to buy a Honda Civic. This can be quite disheartening for any community, making them question the reason why he left Dogecoin behind.

Unfortunately, its fun nature is the primary reason why Dogecoin is popular, and not because of any legitimate innovation that had been created and designed. Many of the social media and news focuses on its joke nature rather than any new and updated design. Dogecoin was actually designed to make fun of the other cryptocurrencies, after all.

But when a market gets saturated with new innovation and software, Dogecoin can very easily fall behind the competition. This leaves the joke and the meme of the cryptocurrency to be the main defender of its popularity. Although it has worked, for now, it is certainly not a guarantee it will work in the future.

There is also way too much dependence on the unpredictable Elon Musk to drive the price as well. Considering his nature and his history, there is no guarantee that Musk will continue promoting Dogecoin. As such, if he were to lose support over one of his choices, comments, or questionable actions (which he does on a frequent basis), the support on Dogecoin itself could be lost. Therefore, it may be best to consider Dogecoin to be a short-term investment instead of a long-term, as there is certainly no certainty about how long it will truly last.

Dogecoin has also received a lot of associations with pump-and-dump schemes. This is where investors pump the crypto with a large number of investments, shooting up the price. Keen investors jump on board in hopes of earning more money. But the same group of investors will quickly sell off their stocks and leave everyone else at a loss and in the dark.

Litecoin

(WorldSpectrum, 2018)

Litecoin is one of the most well-known altcoins, and is often even seen as the silver to Bitcoin's gold. Litecoin is also one of the oldest forms of cryptocurrency around and was published only a mere 2 years after Bitcoin. They were designed by Charlie Lee, a former employee of Google, and Litecoin was actually created to be the lighter version of Bitcoin.

Pros and Cons of Litecoin

Litecoin has faster transaction times than Bitcoin, a high trade volume, as well as good levels of liquidity. Litecoin is also cheaper than Bitcoin, making it a very possible alternative to Bitcoin.

Despite Bitcoin still being the most prominent and popular form of crypto, Litecoin is actually the preferred choice of many professional investors. Considering its high market cap, it has sealed its place in the crypto market.

At least for now, that is.

Litecoin has a better graphic username interface, which means its trading potential is very impressive. Litecoin is also an open-source network, meaning that it is quite easy to implement changes within its protocol. This gives Litecoin the ability to add new innovations and technology to make trading more convenient, and thus likely to stay up to date (perfect for staying ahead of the competition).

Being decentralized gives Litecoin many of the same advantages that Bitcoin holds, meaning there is no reliance on third parties, banks, or any other parties. Because the middleman is removed, you take away the increased risks of manipulation of prices, as well as added security of you staying anonymous.

Litecoin is also fast. This means that any transactions can indeed get processed within 2 to 3 minutes, whereas with Bitcoin it can take up to 10 minutes. For a market that is extremely volatile, this is certainly an added advantage, and the rate of potential attacks for double-spending is also considerably lower.

Litecoin also has lower transaction fees, especially when compared to multiple other cryptocurrencies. This is one of the biggest factors why people started adopting Litecoin.

Litecoin has spared no effort to constantly improve itself, putting a lot of time and effort into making easier transactions and staying on top of its game. Much like any other business, if a coin cannot keep up with the competition, the likelihood of surviving for the long run is slim. Yet Litecoin is one of the oldest cryptocurrencies, and still seems to be running strong.

Litecoin's team has also been proven to be quite trustworthy, where the people are clear and transparent with their goals. This is always ideal for any investment, and certainly means you are able to keep up to date with Litecoin's plans and ideas for the future. Litcoins is also quite a user-friendly platform, making it easier for beginners to start trading.

Almost all hardware wallets do support Litecoin, and it should also be easy to find on most exchanges as well. Thus, working with Litecoin may certainly be less of a problem than many other cryptocurrencies that may be rising to stardom, but are struggling to climb onto the wide variety of exchanges out there.

However, Litecoin has been known to have some branding issues, considering that its name is too close to Bitcoin. Furthermore, the uniqueness that Litecoin had has slowly but surely been declining, with the rise of other altcoins with the same if not at times improved software.

Litecoin has also lost a lot of its credibility over time. Charlie Lee sold his holdings when Litecoin had actually reached a high in 2017, and much like Dogecoin, this delivered a blow to the people who diligently followed Litecoin and its leader.

All in all, there are a large number of pros and cons that are listed for these three different altcoins. It is up to you to decide and consider whether or not they are really worth the investment. Furthermore, if you are interested in investing, it is best to unearth any and all information you can about crypto, looking at both its path, reviews, issues, and more. Just because a cryptocurrency is recommended or popular doesn't mean it is going to be successful. That is the dark side of crypto after all. You never truly know which direction the investment is going to go. All you can do is take some well-researched, thought out, and planned guesses.

Chapter 5: Understanding Altcoin: Ripple, Stellar, and Neo

(rebcenter-moscow, 2017)

Now it is time to take a look at the next set of altcoins you can consider: Ripple, Stellar, and Neo.

Ripple

Ripple stands out because it has a very unique approach as a cryptocurrency. What exactly does this mean? Well, Ripple is unique, because of its new kind of payment protocol, allowing payments to occur and streamline on a global scale.

The Ripple technology does act as a crypto (XRP) as well as a virtual payment network. Chris Larsen and Jed McCaleb are the co-founders, having launched it in 2012, and it is a United States-based company.

Ripple plays three interconnected roles: it works as a network for various different financial transactions, has its own digital currency, and even has a laboratory that is used to develop the Ripple network, other blockchain payments, and XRP.

The idea behind Ripple is to have a more simplified method of payments, considering that many payment systems are both fragmented and quite complicated. This often results in costly payments, as well as extended waiting times, and higher levels of unreliability. Ripple offers a platform that can have international payments, free, and secure, allowing payments to occur with different types of currencies and money, which does include cryptocurrency.

A few years after XRP had been released, Ripple Labs was labeled as one of the 50 smartest companies, and many banks, as well as businesses, have been showing more and more interest in the payment system Ripple had designed.

Pros and Cons of Ripple

Ripple is currently very cheap and affordable, especially for a beginner. But the predictions as to where it may go has been optimistic. So despite its current low price, there is a lot of appeal to where it could go in the near future, and this is what makes it so exciting. Furthermore, being at a lower price means it is a lower investment risk with the potential for higher returns. At the end of the day, you don't have to put as much money into it, and if it doesn't pay off, then the loss will not be that severe.

The market cap of Ripple is about $60 billion, making it currently the fourth biggest crypto in the world. This adds to the level of confidence investors may have in this altcoin, adding to its appeal.

Ripple isn't merely crypto, but also an entire company! This means that it has people marketing the coin as well as public specialists. All in all, there is a group of people dedicated to helping and growing Ripple. Ripple, the company itself has financial backing, even having banking partners to work with. The more banks and financial institutions accept Ripple, the better Ripple will become.

But, keep in mind, Ripple is dealing with a lawsuit. This is where the Securities and Exchange Commission decided to file a high-profile enforcement action against this large company. They made the claims that Ripple sold to them the XRP (Ripple's coin) as a form of unregistered security. Because of Ripple's centralized nature, it should not be qualified as a commodity. The outcome of this lawsuit will really depend on the XRP's contract analyzed by the United States security laws, but so far they are doing well.

However, this resulted in Ripple's price crashing, but the case has actually been shown to be quite weak. Furthermore, Ripple has been making a slow recovery. This proves to be both a benefit and a drawback, as a lawsuit is never good for a company's image, but the fact that it is recovering and the case is weak allows it to show its true strength as well.

Furthermore, Ripple will not be mining any new coins. All the coins have been premined and all of them are currently in circulation. This means that despite demand being pushed up in the future, it will not be able to provide for its means.

Ripple also owns a large amount of XRP itself, where many of the Ripple coins are in the hands of the board members. This means that there is a big chance that Ripple could actually be overinflated because so few people own Ripple.

Ripple is not purely decentralized either, which goes against many of the principles of decentralization and decreased anonymity of users. This is the cause of debate among many as to whether or not Ripple is a true form of crypto, but rather used for the purpose to resolve issues and problems right within the banking industry.

Ripple also has strong competition with SWIFT (a vast messaging network that is normally used by financial institutions, such as banks), and therefore needs to keep ahead in the game by convincing banking sectors their company is safer, as well as having better banking protocols. Either way, having very strong competition means one wrong move could cost them dearly, as well as cost the value of the Ripple coin. This is an area that cannot be well predicted, and you should evaluate yourself whether or not you believe Ripple has got what it takes to succeed and win against the competition.

Furthermore, keep in mind that Ripple and its coin XRP are not actually the same thing. That means that if Ripple succeeds, it may not have a positive benefit to the coin, whereas if the coin succeeds, it might not have a positive effect on the company. Although they are interlinked, sometimes prices may rise and drop regardless of how the company is faring. This is what you need to keep in mind: remember that even if you own some of the coins, you do not own any part of the company.

Ripple certainly has its decent shares of rewards and risks, and it is again up to you to decide whether or not the benefits and the rewards outweigh the risks attached to this cryptocurrency.

Stellar

You can consider Stellar to be a mixed bag, one which aims to serve as a possible universal means of exchange. Thus, the meaning of the name is explained: universal equals universe, and stellar means the stars. Stellar creates the possibility of creating, trading, and sending digital forms of money, such as crypto, dollars, and anything that can work as a digital financial system on a single network.

Stellar disrupts the normal, traditional payment networks, such as the kind that exists in a bank, and allows an average coder and developer to install this system onto their apps for their personal use. To top it off, Stellar is decentralized, adding a great and potential alternative to the normal forms of payment.

However, this prompts the question: Is Stellar's goal actually working? Well, considering that it is one of the top-ranking cryptocurrencies, it has had a lot of success. But it has been around for quite some time and has not necessarily picked up the traction that it should, nor the value of Bitcoin and Ethereum.

Due to certain structural issues, Stellar has had a lot of conflicting predictions, because the project is well funded, but it is dependent on those resources to succeed instead of being self-reliant, in contrast to many of the other cryptocurrencies. So the reality is there is a lot of uncertainty as to whether it will truly be successful or not.

Stellar's coin managed to rise for a brief period to 80 cents in 2017, but then dropped down to a low again in 2018. The next year it took another tumble. So at the current moment, it will take a lot of trader confidence for the price to rise. But considering Bitcoin's ability to double, there would be no surprise if Stellar manages to make it over this hurdle.

There is no indication that the project is doomed, but rather has been focusing on improving and growing, working in conjunction with Ukraine on the digital asset infrastructure. Stellar is also slowly on the rise, but trading with this coin is still volatile, and there is a lot of uncertainty when it comes to this cryptocurrency. Trading volume with stellar has vastly improved, and this is a common yet often disregarded technical parameter that you need to focus on. A rising market is normally indicated by a rising volume. So the fact that Stellar has a rising volume means that its market is slowly but surely growing.

Being decentralized and working closely with Ripple, it has still steered clear of any regulatory body. This is why Stellar and Ripple are different but the same, with Stellar being decentralized by nature and Ripple being centralized. But both have very much the same function, goals, and ideas.

Pros and Cons of Stellar

Stellar's consensus protocol is actually quite a bit faster than other algorithms, reducing both transaction costs and time lags that normally take place in the transactions themselves. Since 2015, it has processed over 450 million different transactions from more than about 5 million different accounts. And it actually processes a few million transactions a day, having the ability to process over a 1,000 to even 5,000 transactions a second.

Stellar is also ahead of Ripple in that it developed a partnership with the government of Ukraine. Having achieved this, Stellar looks to be in line with other partnerships for certain central banks on a global scale. This boosts the potential Stellar actually has over its success, as well as beating the competition in one very important aspect - broadening the potential to connect with other businesses and governments because the steps of partnerships had already been made.

However, Stellar does face a lot of strong competition from Ripple itself, meaning that despite its being a step ahead in the game, it could very easily falter and Ripple can take over. Ripple also has the advantage of more potential customers and easy-to-use software. So Stellar may have to step it up with the innovations in order to truly succeed.

Stellar is still relatively unpopular and not so commonly recognized as many other cryptocurrencies are. Popularity is very important when it comes to boosting investors' confidence. So Stellar will have to work on carving a name for itself in order to really succeed.

There is also a lot of focus on growing Stellar's network, neglecting the much-needed time and effort that should be spent on growing its cryptocurrency. This is probably one of the major reasons why XML (Stellar's coin) still remains largely unpopular.

In comparison to many other cryptocurrency teams, Stellar's team remains quite small. This takes away a lot of potential edges that many other teams have, working together to stay ahead of the game. This means that the rivals already have another advantage Stellar needs to overcome. The best solution would be to build the team.

To put the cherry on top, not many developers are actually interested in Stellar's blockchain. Stellar's offering of a smaller transaction fee could be a benefit for a developer, had Ethereum not taken that step already.

Furthermore, there is no incentive to mine, as there is no need for mining. However, this does mean it cannot draw people in through this method, whereas many more people are attracted to cryptocurrencies because of its mining. It means that Stellar is certainly experiencing less exposure than what other cryptocurrencies are receiving.

Stellar has also shown a large amount of dependency in regards to its price patterns in Bitcoin. Stellar is really struggling to carve out its own niche, which could be detrimental in the long run.

The reason why Stella is so mixed in comparison to others, is because some pros may outweigh the risk in crypto (or at least appear to) and vice versa. But with Stellar, only time will really tell what con may break or what pro may make this cryptocurrency. So it is advised to practice even greater caution with Stellar, and to monitor it on a continuous basis.

Neo

Having been launched in 2014, Neo is commonly called the Chinese Ethereum, where it uses both digital identity and the blockchain to digitize assets. Neo is China's largest form of cryptocurrency, with the same like-minded goals as Ethereum. It allows about 10,000 transactions per second. However, despite its blockchain, Neo is still very centralized in nature in comparison to Ethereum.

Neo means 'new' in Greek; it uses blockchain technology in order to run decentralized applications, such as smart contracts. Neo was also the very first public blockchain project from China.

Pros and Cons of Neo

Smart contracts, digital identities, as well as digital assets are among the main advantages that come with Neo. It has different forms of selling points in comparison to other forms of crypto, thus giving it a competitive edge. Once you use a smart contract, you can digitize any physical asset, meaning that it can remain transparent, traceable, and trustworthy for anyone who registers on the asset.

Neo also has a very strong backing and support from the Chinese government itself, making its potential greater and reducing the likelihood of being shut down due to regulations.

Neo also has a very deep relationship with Onechain. (A software service that focuses on maximizing supply chain performance for retail and manufacturing companies - using planning and deployment algorithms to boost management within a business). They share a similar vision, one which is to be able to perform cross-chain interoperability, hopefully in the very near future. However, in order to achieve this, there has to be a very deep layer of both trust and identity. Where they need to build a middle path is between Onechain's centralized nature and Neo's decentralized pathway.

This means finding a method of dealing with the miners, participants that are transacting, businesses, as well as banks, credit cards, and more.

Some experts have even claimed to be the potential bridge between the two rifts between the two natures of centralized and decentralized. However, this task is monumental, and whether it is even a true possibility without compromising a larger section of one side or the other is a very good question that needs answering.

Should you consider investing in Neo? Well, there is certainly less information about it available compared to other cryptocurrencies. However, it still has the same level of risk as any other cryptocurrency, being volatile by nature.

Furthermore, being partially centralized can again bring trouble for those who believe in and firmly follow decentralized systems. This can be a trouble and a big inhibitor for anyone who wants true anonymity. This is what you really need to consider when considering a cryptocurrency. If it does not meet your goal, then do not invest in it.

Furthermore, Neo does not have a high spot in the market. Although it is one of the biggest cryptocurrencies out there, it is not particularly listed as competing against other cryptos, such as Binance of Cardano. In fact, it is not a well-known cryptocurrency, thus reducing the liquidity and trading volume that comes along with it. Either way, Neo does have a lot of potential for the future, especially if it were to succeed in its emergence against Onechain, thus leaving the possibility open that it could shoot up in popularity after this.

However, this is all speculation, and you may need to do extra research and work into Neo to discover more about it as a cryptocurrency. Considering it is a cryptocurrency in China, there is likely to be more information about it in its original language than what is displayed in the United States or even United Kingdom news. This means that you may need to face a potential language barrier from time to time in order to receive the necessary updates to stay as current, as you would with many of the other cryptocurrencies.

At the end of the day, you will have to do your own work and research into these cryptocurrencies before making the final choice. A lot of the information is dense, allowing you to see both sides of crypto as well as teaching you about what you need to look out for. As a beginner, the more research you do on your investment choices the better, as it is far more likely to keep you out of trouble and in the loop.

Chapter 6: Understanding Altcoin: Tether, Binance, and Cardano

Tether, Binance, and Cardano are the last batch left. You may by now have realized how appealing the advantages may sound, only to be struck by the drawbacks. In essence, there is no way of truly knowing which way a cryptocurrency will head toward, only that eventually, the benefits might outweigh the drawbacks or the drawbacks might eventually kill the crypto or drag it down.

This is where you have to assess and decide which way you think it will go, as there is no sure way of knowing. You will have to make the final choice, and accept the future when it reveals the final success or failure.

Tether

Tether, or USDT, is actually quite a unique cryptocurrency that is actually tied to a specific fiat currency (USD or US dollars) in order to create a certain level of stability. The currency was created in order to confront three major challenges, in hopes of remedying them.

First, Tether hoped to bring the ability to transfer national currency; second, it hoped to enable a more stable Bitcoin, and third, it hoped to create options for checking.

Tether Limited is actually based in Hong Kong, and serves as a third party for the crypto currency's assets. It does hold a certain amount of USD in order to have the same amount of USDT in circulation. This is a simple plan that erases a lot of the complexity involved in running certain fiat or crypto audits. There is still complete transparency that comes with the audits.

Pros and Cons of Tether

Transactions happen literally within minutes. This is very beneficial, especially for traders who enjoy the ability to trade at a moment's notice. However, when USD deposits are made with the bank themselves, it can take a couple of days.

There is certainly the additional advantage of stability, as many exchanges are actually open to the idea of taking Tether, but not fiat currencies. This could also play to your advantage if you are someone who likes to play it safe.

The transaction charges 0n Tether involve almost no fees in comparison to SWIFT transfers, making Tether quite an ideal platform for online and financial transfers. With stability, there is less risk when you are waiting for the right opportunity on the exchanges. Again, this is ideal for someone who is less inclined to make risky choices.

However, on the flip side, it does lack the anonymity that many cryptocurrencies boast of. You will be required to bring documents, verifying your identity, before you will have the right to purchase Tether. For people who use cryptocurrency for its privacy, this makes Tether as a cryptocurrency a no-go.

There is also the price stability that can work as a disadvantage, because although it has goals to remain the same price as fiat currency, fiat prices do not remain the same, making their claims untrue at times. There is always a small level of volatility, about 2% to 3%, but it will never be able to reach the perfect zero that a lot of people see as ideal.

Furthermore, no mining really takes place with Tether. There is no option and only the business that runs Tether can actually do this. It is likely to add to the uniformity and keep its value in line with the US dollar, thus it cannot draw in the popularity and numbers from digital miners, which is an unfortunate disadvantage.

Binance

Keep in mind, Binance is an exchange platform as well as having its own cryptocurrency. Later in the chapter, we will address the advantages of using the exchange platform in Chapter 9, but now the focus is on the coin itself.

The Binance coin was created in 2017, but Binance itself was actually launched first on the Ethereum platform, then afterward moved to its own blockchain. And it actually only took weeks before it raised about $15 million. This was used to build up the platform and emergency funds have been set aside.

The Binance coin does have a limited amount of 200 million, with over a million already in circulation.

The primary goal of the Binance coin is the idea to create easier transactions and also give people the motivation to keep them on their platform. There is a discount when you use the Binance coin to trade on their platform, so for anyone who wants to cut their trading fees, this is certainly an option.

Pros and Cons of Binance

The Binance coin's popularity comes with it's exchange platform (which is the second top cryptocurrency exchange in the world), due to its strong and large exchange platform backing. Binance coins are certainly one of the best utility tokens a person can use and can be used to trade and also pay fees on its very popular platform. It can also be used for various other payment systems, outside of the exchanges and companies, making it an appealing choice for investments, considering other companies trust in its value.

Binance also has a very interesting burn policy (where coins are moved to dud accounts effectively removing them from use, such as is done with real currencies and bank notes), helping to ensure Binance's growth as well as stability. Anything that can help grow the profits and stability of a volatile cryptocurrency is naturally quite a good advantage to have.

Binance also acts as a form of discount coupon. Playing as a marketing agent to spur loyalty to a large exchange platform gives a large boost to its popularity. There is the incentive of having discounts for fees when using the coin on the trading platform.

Binance, the trading platform, is also very popular, breeding the largest form of crypto exchanges that have the largest number of crypto pairs available.

To top it off, Binance had an excellent response to security breaches, building the trust of traders rather than weakening people's resolve to use the platform.

The smart chain on Binance had the same amount of potential to beat Ethereum. Now that is quite a competitive advantage to have! The smart chain did not actually garner much attention when it was launched in 2020, but in 2021 it has been given the spotlight. At the same time, Ethereum's fees had started to climb; therefore, it has the potential to take over. That in itself shows high potential for the coin itself.

However, because Binance is actually a company, it does mean that it is heavily centralized. This immediately takes over a lot of the anonymity and goes against many avid cryptocurrency supporters, who want to take the world away from the traditional, centralized banking systems.

This means there are many regulators who actually want to take Binance down. Many securities and finance commissions are working against Binance, potentially breaking it down just as it reaches its highest peak. Binance was warned by Germany for installing tracker tokens. Then it got into trouble with Japan by not being allowed to regulate there. This was also not their first time Binance has had issues in Japan.

The biggest blow occurred when the United Kingdom actually completely banned Binance.

Binance had also been a target of large-scale cyber attacks. There was an unsuccessful attempt in 2018, but in 2019 another attack occurred in which the hackers walked away with over 7,000 BTC. Despite Binance's strong response, many investors could be concerned that a security breach occurred.

Binance is also in heavy competition against other cryptocurrencies.

Although it has been shown that Binance has actually been stealing a lot of the spotlight from Ethereum, even Ethereum's own new design could take back the spotlight. Not only does this mean it can pull ahead, but it can also knock the cryptocurrency back quite a few steps. So it is best to monitor both Binance and Ethereum to understand who is truly winning in this game.

And Ethereum is not the only concern. Cardano has also been rising in the ranks, coming close to launching its own smart contracts, and has been advancing very far as well. This means that more and more crypto are competing against each other, fighting to take the next spot when the opportunity does happen to present itself.

Cardano

Cardano is the first peer-reviewed network as well as open-source software in existence. It does aim to deliver any form of advanced features that are found from research and scientific-based processes.

Cardano was created in Hong Kong by Charles Hoskinson, who used to be a former founder of Ethereum. He had also worked with Ethereum Classic and Bitshares.

In the beginning, academic specialists were assigned to review Cardano's protocol. The main goal was to create a great third-generation platform that can boost the improvement of deployments of smart contracts, as well as continue to resolve the scaling issues that Bitcoin seems to have, which is the first generation that is existing at this point in time. That is why many people ponder the potential Cardano has to fulfill the promise of or even replace Bitcoin, which is quite a goal to consider.

Pros and Cons of Cardano

Cardano is a cryptocurrency that is built out of two layers. This unique idea was what boosted its popularity when it first started out. One layer is used to specifically deal with the transactions, having very small transaction fees tagged to it. The second layer is meant to run smart contracts, as well as decentralized apps.

Cardano has also been proven to be quite environmentally friendly, not taking as much electricity when people work to mine it. Furthermore, the transactions are known to be faster due to its processing and scalable consensus mechanism. Bitcoin and Ethereum had been receiving a lot of flak from all the energy needed in order to mine them, but Cardano is exempt from this flak, adding to its popular reputation. Cardano also has a great development team in and of itself. This means it grew a lot of popularity purely from its co-founders and because it had been peer-reviewed, it reflected no true weakness in the protocol itself. It developed many of the protocols itself. Having focused on developing an advanced blockchain in order to fight against hacks as well as bugs.

Cardano's native coins are called ADA and have a total limited supply of about 45 billion coins. It is a very attractive asset in various different financial industries, because it makes use of the double layers, allowing for unlimited amounts of scalability, and quick transactions.

Cardano also has academic backing, which is a unique advantage. In fact, many academics have written papers that propose other methods or steps Cardano can take in order to improve itself. This adds a level of credibility to its design, allowing people to trust it far more than others.

An open-source platform is also an advantage worth considering. It is written in the Haskell programming language, which is completely open-source and allows for a higher level of transparency.

Cardano is a quieter, secure form of blockchain, with a great protocol and mathematically proven safety. Security is becoming more and more important in this modern day and age, and being able to see Cardano's secure nature does allow for more comfort when considering investing in this coin.

Cardano has provided a means of digital identity, even to citizens who do not have access to banks. Despite being decentralized, it has this capability, making it more popular even in the more rural areas of the globe.

Perhaps because of this, Cardano has been gaining a global presence in Africa, where they encourage people on the continent to use this app by resolving issues that can be solved with blockchain technology. They certainly had success in Ethiopia, having made the biggest blockchain deal in any country. By boosting its popularity in the third world, it takes up the potential to grow in popularity on a global scale.

Even companies have taken a vast interest in this cryptocurrency, many of them switching from Etherum to Cardano. This means yhat Cardano is gaining traction and a comfortable footing in regards to its overall competition.

Cardano is also listed on Coinbase, which is a huge achievement for a cryptocurrency. Coinbase is very careful with the coins they choose and decide to list. So the fact that Cardano qualifies in their books is a great reflection. The availability of Cardano on Coinbase does make it easier for traders to use and purchase it, making it already more popular.

In the first 2 months of 2021, the value of Cardano has risen to over 221% according to Trading Education Team, 2021, reaching an all-time high. It has even, if only for a temporary while, taken third place in the world's largest cryptocurrencies. Although it did fall back, it shows the amount of potential this cryptocurrency really has.

Unfortunately, Cardano is still in development. This means there is a lot this platform can still do to improve and innovate. This is the primary reason why it is still losing against the fully formed Ethereum, as it is still working with incomplete smart contracts at the end of the day. In fact, Cardano does not have the smart contract capabilities functioning at the moment. This is likely to be one of the greatest hindrances towards it's growth, as a function is only useful once it has been launched, not spoken about. And until the smart contracts are actually launched, a person cannot altogether rely on the promises that it has given.

Cardano also wants to implement a form of voting system. This can work all well and good, except that many of the traders are inexperienced, thus the votes can take a turn in a biased direction, allowing Cardano to make choices that are not altogether wise, just because the voters really don't know better.

Multichains (a cryptocurrency that runs on more than one blockchain) are also an old concept, with many other cryptocurrencies having boarded this technology train and designed their own. This means the unique advantage Cardano used to have has now been eliminated, and it may have to strive for different and new innovations to keep up with the competition (thus the issue with the underdeveloped smart contracts as well). If it keeps running behind, it will be overall detrimental for Cardano's growth, because as quickly as it rose to popularity, it can also fallt.

Charles Hoskinson himself is at a disadvantage because of his controversial nature, especially with the way he interacts and communicates with people online. He has had to backtrack on quite a few inflammatory comments he had made, as well as having a falling out with important people. Furthermore, it is hard to take him altogether seriously, which is never good for a company. A business needs to have a strong leader and one that stands on what he says. Much like Elon Musk, Hoskinson is certainly unpredictable, which does not work in Cardano's favor.

There has also been quite suspicious marketing of Cardano that had taken place in Japan. This adds a certain layer of suspicion, as well as insecurity about what was really taking place, putting Cardano in a different light.

And despite what others may really say, Cardano will still remain a high-risk investment because of its cryptocurrency nature. All it takes is one wrong step and things can fall flat for this unique crypto, and much like anything else, it is up to you to decide whether or not the rewards outweigh the risks.

These are some of the top cryptocurrencies that are listed in 2021. Keep in mind, things can change within months or a year, and it is recommended that you keep up to date with which cryptocurrency is actually faring better than the others. No one can truly guarantee one crypto's success, nor can one really see the end of another crypto coming. All you can do is monitor the currencies, keep up to date with the trends, as well as any and all news that relates to a cryptocurrency. Again, you have to make the choice, and you have to take responsibility in order to ever have hope of making a profit.

Chapter 7: Understanding Safety and Security

If you have been working online and learning about cryptocurrency, there is one common danger that keeps rearing its ugly head: scams. This results in loss caused by fraud and the actions of others, and has nothing to do with the way of the market. Scams are probably one of the worst ways to lose money, and with crypto, the likelihood of recovering or even catching the scammers is very slim, if not impossible, depending on the scam.

So the best way to tackle this problem is to work to avoid it in the first place. Aversion is a clever strategy, and as a beginner, you are more vulnerable to scams. This is why it is best for you to prepare yourself from the very beginning to stay as safe as possible. The worst forms of losses are the ones that could have been completely avoided.

First, when you are looking into various cryptocurrency companies, it is best to confirm that they are indeed powered by blockchain. This means they have publicly available data on all the transactions that are taking place. You can also double-check that the business plans they have are solid and actually work to resolve real and legitimate problems (thus having a background history on how businesses should work yourself is not altogether a bad idea.)

Basically, here are a few things to look out for (most common scams) and methods to avoid becoming the victim as you start your journey in cryptocurrency.

(aitoff, 2016)

Fake Websites

Following a tip by someone you trust is not uncommon, but you can become a victim by landing on the wrong/fake website. There are a huge number of fake digital websites on the web that look very close, if not identical, to the original and valid startup companies. You can check the authenticity by verifying whether the small lock icon is actually next to the URL bar, and whether or not there is an '"HTTPS" on the site (a fake website commonly has an HTTP, whereas a legitimate website has an HTTPS).

Be aware, even if a site genuinely looks authentic, be careful if you still find yourself visiting other platforms when you need to pay. Attackers sometimes create a website link switching out the letter 'o' with a zero - making it almost impossible to tell the difference.

In essence, just be careful with the sites you visit. Paranoia when it comes to the web is far more likely to pay off. By just making the extra check, you can save yourself a lot of time, trouble and money.

Fake Mobile Apps

This is a common trick that scammers use when it comes to cryptocurrency. They upload fake apps, even in stores such as Apple App and the Google Play Store. Normally, these apps are very quickly called out, but that doesn't mean you can't fall for their traps from time to time.

According to Bitcoin News, thousands of people have downloaded cryptocurrency apps that are fake. And if you are an Android user, you tend to be at a greater risk. It is always a good idea to check the app you are downloading. Check the branding and the design. If it looks inauthentic or even has strange coloring, avoid it. Do you see any forms of misspellings or is the logo incorrect? Then you really need to reconsider downloading the app. Remember, if you can, to also check the reviews. People tend to be quite verbal when they are unhappy, and the review slot is proof of that.

Tweets and Social Media Updates

There is a big reason why social media should not be used as authentic and reliable. These sites are filled with scammers, hackers, or more. If you have a knack of following celebrities, make sure you are following legitimate and verified accounts instead of a fan/imposter account. Impersonating bots run rampant, and could easily post to people to try out different crypto links or companies under the guise of a trusted celebrity. This can mislead many people. So do not trust the offers or news that come from Twitter or Facebook. Everyone should know by now that Facebook is a haven for fake news.

Even if someone asks for a very small amount of crypto on these platforms for whatever reason, the likelihood is high you are never getting it back. And just because other people are replying positively to the offer does not mean it is legitimate either. The same person can own multiple accounts!

Email Scammers

If you receive an email, and it looks like it comes from a legitimate crypto company, be very careful before diving in and investing. Does the email look identical to the branding and logo of the company? Is it possible to verify the email address from the original company's website? If you have doubts, see if you can contact the people from the company you are interested in, to verify. But never ever click a link directly from the email that leads you to a site. This is because you can open a doorway for malware and viruses to enter your computer. So you don't even have to fill in your banking details to lose out. Rather, they can get access to all your private information digitally, and worse yet, steal the coins in your ewallet.

Scammers love to announce the false ICO (initial coin offerings) as a method to steal a large number of funds. Make sure to always double-check the emails, and even consider using an antivirus weblink scanner if you are unsure about the site you would like to visit.

There are still many ways and tricks scammers use to try and steal from you online. Consider boosting your online digital security by getting an advanced antivirus program and using VPN when browsing the internet. An average scammer or hacker will go for easy targets, considering they are less work and effort. So you are significantly reducing your risks of becoming a victim by putting a little extra effort to your overall online security.

Common Bitcoin Scams

Considering that Bitcoin still happens to be the most common form of cryptocurrency out there, it is no wonder that Bitcoin is also the most common target for scams. Being aware of these scams can help you become aware of other scams in another cryptocurrency that could arise or have already been developed.

Exchanges and Wallet Hacks

Normally, cryptocurrency exchanges used to be the primary target point for hackers, but now they have decided to turn their attention to other potential hotspots, such as online wallets. One of the biggest hacks occurred in June 2020, where a hacker had stolen about a million email addresses of customers by breaking into the databases ledger for email and marketing databases. They had also stolen the personal details of 9,500 customers and ended up publishing 242,000 email addresses of customers of the website that had a hacker's database (Liebkind, 2020). The wallet was called Ledger, which happened to be a France-based company of crypto wallets. Each and every one of the customers had to be persuaded to change their passwords. Poloniex, a crypto exchange market, had suffered a similar fate in 2019. So be very careful of the online wallets and exchanges you choose, and change your passwords frequently.

Social Engineering Scams

This is when hackers use psychological manipulation and deceit in order to get vital information from user accounts. Phishing is a common example, where hackers send emails to their targets, linking them to a fake website in order to gather important information, such as personal details and bank account information.

Phishing scams target information that tends to pertain to the online wallets when it comes to cryptocurrency. Hackers are normally very keen on getting their hands on a person's private keys. Private keys are used to access the funds that are inside the wallets. The tactics used are quite similar to the standard scams. An email leads people to a designed website asking them to place in the information of their private keys. This way they can steal Bitcoin or any other cryptocurrency that lies within those wallets.

ICO Scams

(Tumisu, 2021)

ICO scams became quite a prevalent and concerning situation from 2017 to 2018. However, there was a massive crackdown on the Security Exchange Commission (SEC), and the amount of ICO scams has significantly decreased. But they have never died down completely, and you still need to be very careful. The federal agency is still working to crack down on these scams.

There are a variety of methods that scammers can use to steal Bitcoin from investors. Normally fake websites are a popular method, and even the ICO itself could be the problem. ICO could distribute the tokens that find the loopholes of the security laws, or even be misleading investors through the creation of false advertisements.

One of the most popular examples/warnings is when Centra Tech was actually backed by a large number of celebrities, including Floyd Mayweather and even DJ Khaled. When the regulatory agency caught them, however, many of them were penalized and some even faced jail time.

DeFi Rug Pulls

This is quite a new scamming strategy that has hit the cryptocurrency markets. This is when DeFi (decentralized finance) focuses on removing the gatekeepers of financial transactions. But this comes with it's own massive set of issues. Such bad actors have managed to get away with the funds of investors using these avenues. It is a practice that is normally called a 'rug pull.' Normally, what happens is a project is designed with the promise of great returns. The money is kept 'safe' in smart contracts. But programmers find ways to steal the fund after the contract expires or actually reaches the threshold limit, making use of the functions on the DeFi platform.

In December 2020, a group of developers stole almost $750,000 worth of Bitcoin and other cryptocurrencies. The project had promised to deposit their crypto in a locked smart contract, and the contract could only be executed after a very specific period of time. But the developers had developed and built in a back door and made away with the funds long before the smart contract had even expired.

Beginner Mistakes to Avoid

Apart from scams, one of the biggest ways losses occur is through mistakes. As a beginner, you are bound to make a few, and it is best to actually avoid them where you can. *Knowledge* is when you learn from your mistakes, but it classifies as *wisdom* when you learn from the mistakes of others. Avoiding these mistakes allows you to reduce a lot of the risk involved in investing in crypto.

Do Not Anthropomorphize the Crypto Market

Remember, the market does not have any human qualities to it at all. It consists of numbers, figures, and logic. It works on a lot of software programs and artificial intelligence. Yet, many people end up talking about the market as if it has an agency. This gives an illusion to people about how the market actually works, but it all ends up being a misunderstanding. The market happens to be the sum of all economic transactions. It is not some entity that you are actually competing against. When you personify or humanize a market, you are playing a short hand and working at a disadvantage. This might seem like an odd mistake to make, but it is very common.

To add to this, many people grow an emotional connection to a specific market, and this is what you need to avoid at all costs. Gaining an emotional connection, whether through a lot of research or working with the company, can cause you to hold on longer than you should, or fall into common scams and traps.

Diversify

The saying "don't put all your eggs in one basket" is a suitable cliche that you should follow. The idea of diversifying is not a new concept. This is because it is known to work. You are far more likely to lose everything if you bet it all in one place. This is true for any market, especially crypto. You should consider diversifying, as it really doesn't hurt to add some variety into your portfolio, regardless of the benefits of spreading the risks.

Skills Trump Chance

Although luck has handed people their fair share of fortunes, you can consider trading to have more in common with chess than a roll of the dice. Trading does require you to possess common knowledge that is up to date. You need to be well-read and in touch with the news, instead of waiting on your lucky star. The more work you put into trading, the better luck may find its way to you. You don't get lucky by blindly trading. You get lucky by working for it and weighing the odds in an informed way. Remember, skill comes from being informed, and when entering the crypto market you need to do your homework before investing.

Avoid Peer Pressure

Peer pressure exists all across the world and social media, but idly following the trends and calls of the pressure in crypto is a massive mistake, because by the time people let you know of something that has potential, it is normally too late. You are more likely to make a loss when you jump in late to a trend, despite it being the advice of others. It is okay to miss out sometimes, as long as you play it safe. Furthermore, many people unintentionally pull others into investment schemes, such as the pyramid scheme, and you should avoid them as well.

There is nothing wrong with listening to advice and getting critique, but at the end of the day, you have to be confident in your own choice. Independence is critical to boosting your success.

There Are No Such Things as Oracles

Everyone believes they are an expert in a topic until proven wrong. There are many self-proclaimed seers, but no matter how many webinars they host or blogs they post, it never adds up to complete certainty. Take everything you hear and read with a little more skepticism. Because no matter what, even if these people are successful, they will always be holding back a small truth to keep you from fully making it, kind of like holding out one tiny part of a recipe. Or they share what worked for them when in reality it was just luck. So although it is good to learn from them, a careful balance needs to be created. Filtering the lies and the truth whether by verifying them or making logical deductions. This is a sad reality. As much as the internet and people are a wealth of information, there are also a lot of scams/liars out there to either boost their own ego or get your money. But there are also people interested in helping you succeed. It is best to find those who have better intentions in mind, and stick with them in the long run.

Panic Selling

In order to trade professionally, you need to have a strong stomach, especially in a market whose price movements are rapid and unpredictable, such as in cryptocurrency. A common beginner mistake is selling the moment the market seems to be getting a little rough. Sometimes it is a valid choice, where you want to cut your losses as soon as possible, but technically it isn't a loss until you sell below value. If there are some promising indicators, perhaps it is better to hold on to the investment as it could push up again. You really don't want to have to buy it at a high point and sell it at a low. This is literally giving your money away, which is the exact opposite of your goal as a trader. What you want is the approach called HODL, which stands for *hold on for dear life* while waiting for the market to recover.

Exiting Too Late

Another common mistake is being clueless after you have actually made a profit. You don't want to hold on to an investment until it is actually too late. So, you need to learn the balance of buying and selling at the right times. You are bound to get it wrong from time to time, but experience can help you compensate for a lot of it.

Jealousy

Jealousy is a dangerous emotion and it is normally a bad idea to trade while emotional, but jealousy is by far worse. Never engage in trading because of someone else's success, considering it really has nothing to do with you. This emotion can not only affect how you trade badly, but also how you react around others who might be doing better than you. It is also an emotionally draining activity that can prevent you from discovering many opportunities. So in short, it is best to leave jealousy alone, and instead find joy in someone else's win. After all, you could truly learn from it too.

Building Your Own Digital Vault

When it comes to spammers and hackers, you will want to build your own personal digital vault to keep your cryptocurrency safe, especially with the rise of hackers and scammers that have now decided to target Bitcoin and crypto due to the growth in popularity. There is no doubt that in this day and age, cybercrime is on the rise, and when you want to entrust your money online, you want to do everything you can to keep it safe.

Start off by working with reputable online wallets, brokerages, exchanges, and mobile apps. You do not owe new businesses or startups anything. Go for what has been tried and true. Before making use of any form of a platform, do some research on how your data will be protected. Check its history, and see whether or not it has faced hacks before. Companies and platforms need to add the best features, such as adding multifactor authentication and having wallets stored offline. Using more than one platform can also prove to be safe, and design complex passwords for every software requiring you to log in. But, make absolutely sure you do not lose your passwords (even consider using a password manager).

Many people use the crypto wallets on their mobile phones, but don't add the proper securities to their devices. Many hackers focus on targeting the mobile device, using mobile phishing campaigns to get enough personal information. You should consider installing antivirus software on your phone, as this device is as much of a target as your computer is.

Be very careful how you use your wallet in transactions. Be cyber-resilient in your wallet. Cyberattacks are staged and planned to try to get a foothold. So be very aware of the process of your digital wallet, and how it can be used in transactions. Change the password on a regular basis. Preferably, do not connect on public wifi, and be very careful of what happens with your wallet.

There are certainly a large variety of processes and steps you can take to protect the digital currency you own. The responsibility of your crypto lies completely in your hands, so learn about secret key protection, crypto miner malware protection, and recovery seed protection (hardware wallets that are both generated randomly and stored offline in the microprocessors of the device-meaning if your device does get infected, all your recovery seeds and crypto assets will remain secure).

Furthermore, avoid sharing your secret key. This is used to validate the person who is either sending or receiving digital coins. The secret key, also called the private key, should never be shared with anyone. It is even best to store your secret key in cold storage or offline wallets, as this is the safest place to keep it. When you use cold storage, you are actually printing it out, then wiping any and all digital traces of the key. However, it does mean that you have to keep it safe and private in the physical world.

It is best to avoid wallets that are normally hosted by providers. They are essentially the worst choice because it means placing your private key in their server and out of your control. It means it is at higher risk of getting lost because of a breach, the provider even losing the business, or having a takeover of the infrastructure by another legal entity or perhaps even the government.

Taking a Peek at Different Wallets

It is important to understand the different types of digital wallets that are available for your use. There are three primary wallets.

First is the closed wallet or desktop wallet, which allows users to be the only ones able to use the funds that are stored and retrieved. Closed wallets are offline, meaning that they are certainly more secure; but because of this, it does take more time to perform the transactions, which is not ideal for anyone who is very active with their investments.

Second are the mobile wallets, where the largest difference from the closed wallet lies in the fact that you store the data/keys on your phone via a mobile application. It offers far more flexibility in that you can be anywhere as you exchange your funds, and even use QR codes that adds to the convenience of buying and selling crypto. However, it does have some security issues, as you need to make sure your mobile phone remains virus-free.

Third are hardware wallets. This is where your keys are saved on a physical device and are not connected to the internet, removing the vulnerability of hackers. It is important to create a seed phrase to ensure that if you lose your device you can still gain access to your crypto. Even when you work with transactions, the private key you have will never leave the device itself. It works on validating the data and requesting the transaction details, making it infinitely more secure.

In summary, the tips to reduce the risks in cryptocurrency are by practicing trading psychology, always being suspicious of news or messages until proven wrong, and doing your research. The majority of the time, taking that extra 5 minutes to Google a topic or business can allow you to reveal its true identity. In 5 minutes you can determine, for the most part, what are scams and what are legitimate. The scary reality is that not many people practice this craft, and end up falling for a scam that is clearly declared so on the web. The worst losses are those that could have been avoided. So be a savvy trader and learn to avoid them.

Chapter 8: Understanding Investment Strategies

Anyone who has taken on a sport knows that they don't immediately dive headfirst into a game hoping to win. In fact, if this were to occur, you would basically be setting yourself up to lose, and miserably so. Yet many traders tend to walk into this method of practice without even thinking twice, often to their detriment.

Furthermore, although I recommend that you build your own strategies, this does not mean you don't have to follow others when you start off. In fact, it can certainly be recommended to start off and learn from the strategies of others before jumping in and creating your own.

Paper Trading

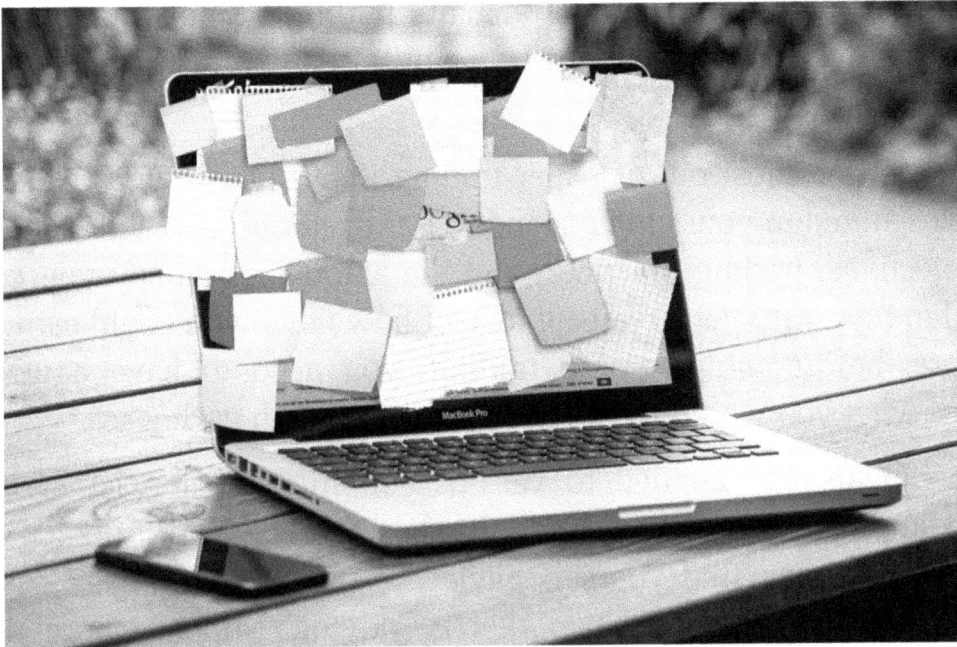

(geralt, 2018)

First, it is best to be introduced to the practice ground of a trader/investor. This is commonly called paper trading or a simulated trade. A paper trade normally allows investors and traders to practice buying and selling without actually having to risk any of their money. The term itself derives from back in history, where people aspiring to trade practiced on paper before risking any of their money in live markets.

This is ideal when you are a beginner and have little to no experience. This allows you to understand the fundamentals of trade, learn how to read charts and portfolios, different trading positions, and the making of both profits or losses. On average, most people practice trading using an electronic market simulator. It looks almost identical to the authentic trading platforms out there. The closer the simulator is to real life, the better practice and experience you can indeed receive.

Paper Trading Revelations

Online paper trading platforms have been growing in popularity as their design has become more user-friendly and realistic. In fact, investors can even participate in 'live trades' without actually putting a single penny into them. This allows investors to learn how to analyze the real markets without actually risking their money.

A good way to get the most out of paper trading is by focusing on realistic trading scenarios suited to your circumstances. For example, you will want to follow real objectives, trading practices, and the amount of money you can actually afford to invest (to get a realistic idea of how much you could earn or lose). Therefore, before jumping into trading, you need to have a well-founded idea of what you would like to accomplish through trading.

Paper trading can also be applied to various conditions that exist in the market. For example, if you place a trade that has higher volatility (such as cryptocurrency), you may find yourself having to deal with slippage costs that are higher because of how the market is moving. Slippage normally occurs when the trader gains a different price in the trade than that which was predicted.

However, you may ask, "What is the difference between a paper trading account and a live account?" First, paper trading eliminates the risk of danger, thus building up a false sense of security, which can in the end result in bad or even distorted returns on investment.

Second, because it reduces the risk, paper trading cannot prepare you for the emotional toll of an investment, which can only be learned when real money is at stake.

Finally, paper trading may not manage to take all the costs and fees into consideration. which is what you will have to do when setting a budget. Paper trading covers a lot, but still does not fully manage to cover everything that is generally expected in actual trading.

Still, this is an excellent training ground, and any drawback is minimal in comparison to all the benefits it can bring.

Investment Strategies for a Beginner

Cryptocurrency investments are risky. That is a fact and one you will hear often when it comes to crypto. When you trade without a plan, it is likely to lead to a loss on your part. As the saying goes: if you fail to plan then you are planning to fail. All in all, there is no absolute perfect trading strategy that has been designed. But there are three popular methods that are quite suitable for beginners, and therefore something you should consider in order to build experience.

In order to achieve these strategies, you will need an online charting tool and a foundation knowledge of candlestick charts. There are some free online charting tools available, such as Yahoo Finance, StockCharts, or even Tradingview. It is all up to you, with what you are comfortable with using. Maybe try out different platforms until you find the one you enjoy the most. Before tackling the three strategies, we first need to explain candlestick charts, so that you have a good grasp of what you need to accomplish.

Candlestick Charts

Traders and investors alike need to have the ability to analyze price action, and the candlestick charting style is a handy tool for this. The candlestick is a representative of price activity that occurs with an asset over a very specific period of time. The candlestick consists of four main components: the open, low, high, and close.

The 'open' part of the candlestick is a representation of the price of the asset when the trading had actually begun, and the 'close' is a reflection of the conclusion of the price for that specific time period. The 'low' and the 'high' reflect the lowest as well as the highest prices that are achieved.

Each candlestick also has two features physically displayed, which consist of the four main components. The first feature is called the 'body,' which happens to be the wide middle section of the candlestick. It normally acts as a reflection of the observation period during its open and close.

The close is normally shown on the top of the body of the candlestick, when it is green, or at the bottom of the candlestick, when it is red. It is vice versa for the open, where it is situated at the top of the body of a green candlestick, and down at the bottom for a red candlestick. The final two components, high and low, are reflected on the secondary feature, which is normally called the 'wick' as it displays two thin lines, one at the top and one at the bottom. The high and low are represented in the same way. where the high is on the very top tip of the wick in the green candle and at the very bottom of the wick on a red candle, and vice versa for the low on the candles.

In the end, any candle that is green has a higher price at the end than the beginning price when it ended, and is red if the beginning price is higher than the ending price.

Many cryptocurrency traders take advantage of this market by using this chart over the course of daytime frames. A candlestick normally represents 1 to 4 hours and can even go up to 12 hours. If you intend to invest in the long term, you may want to choose candlesticks that represent days, weeks, or possibly even months.

Normally a candlestick becomes bullish when it is green and bearish when it is red, and this is particularly useful for anyone forming strategies on the bull and bear markets.

Diving Into Strategy

Dollar-Cost Averaging

Dollar-cost averaging (DCA) is a very popular and time-tested trading strategy. It generally works better over extended periods of time. The idea of it is quite simple as well. Rather than investing all the money you set aside into specific crypto, you will divide it into smaller amounts. Then you will choose a specific time and day during the week where you will buy the cryptocurrency. And you are only allowed to buy them at those times.

For instance, Harry wants to invest $20,000 in Bitcoin. But he decides to take on the DCA strategy, and he divides the money into 20 lots of $1,000. Then he decides on a particular day and time, such as Friday at 3 p.m., and purchases Bitcoin every single week at that time until he has invested the entire amount.

When you purchase crypto at extended periods of time at regular intervals, you actually help to reduce the negative impact you may have with market volatility, the prices rising and falling at a rapid pace. This means Harry is very likely to receive more Bitcoin because of this purchasing strategy, as opposed to having spent it all in 1 day.

You can investigate this strategy a little further by using DCABT, which is a Bitcoin-focused calculator, focusing on the DCA strategy and demonstrating this point in greater detail.

Golden Cross/Death Cross

This trading strategy uses a tactic where you express two moving averages (MAs), which is the chart indicator line that displays the mean average price of an asset over a certain period of time. When you use this strategy, you tend to look for crossovers that range between 50 MA (an average of the last 50 days) and 200 MA (the average of the past 200 days). You can use this on daily or even weekly charts, and considering this takes a lot of time and research, it is more of a long-term trading strategy.

There are two kinds of crossovers you want to keep an eye out for: convergence (golden cross), which occurs when the 50 MA crosses above the 200 MA; and divergence (death cross), which occurs when the 50 MA crosses below the 200 MA.

Convergence normally acts as an indicator of short-term momentum that surpasses the long-term momentum and is traditionally the signal for you to buy. When the opposite occurs, (divergences), this is normally an indicator that you need to sell. Divergences normally occur when a huge number of traders leave the market and are busy selling their assets.

In order to properly set up this chart, you will need to work with your online charting tool account and change the time frame you want to either daily or weekly. Use the indicator button to search for 'moving averages.' When you click twice, you can add two MAs.

RSI Divergence Crypto Trading Strategy

This is a more technical strategy that is great when it comes to timing trend reversals right before they occur. RSI means Relative Strength Index. This is a chart indicator that tends to monitor momentum by working out the average amount of gains and losses that have occurred over a 2-week period. The indicator line works between 0 and 100 and can point out when an asset is actually being oversold or over purchased.

When a channel (when the price of an asset moves between two parallel trendlines) is between 30 and 70, it reflects the normal average. When an asset extends beyond 70, it is an indicator that it is being overbought, whereas below 30 it is considered to be oversold. When it is oversold, the price is far more likely to rise when it is being overbought (where the price is likely to drop).

However, despite the promises of this system, it can at times give deceiving results, so even if the price shows that the asset is being oversold, the price may drop down even further. The best way to discern this is by looking at the discrepancies that can occur between the RSI indicator and the price. If it is working well, both the RSI indicator and the price normally follow the same patterns, but when the price falls and the RSI rises or the other way round, it is normally an indication that there truly is a shift in buying or purchasing volume.

At the end of the day, there are several other strategies you can consider taking on if you want to. Just make sure you take your time to do the research necessary, and that you understand your plan of action before proceeding. Test these strategies out on paper trading as a practice ground before jumping into real trading, as it may give you confidence and certainly a better idea of whether you are even implementing the strategies in the correct way.

Consider getting yourself a mentor who likes to implement strategies and target trades similar to the ones you are interested in. You can certainly learn a lot from those who have had more experience in the trading field and have achieved success. However, avoid the temptation of copy-catting a successful trader's work. This is because the time and circumstances they had when making specific choices will not have the same results when you make those decisions. Furthermore, be careful of trading gurus and webinars. As much as you believe you could learn something from them, even if it is strategies, keep in mind they always give just enough information for you to be dangerous, but not enough for you to be altogether successful. That success hangs more in your hands and your decisions, and the flow of the market, because even the most intelligent person cannot altogether predict the future, nor which way the market may actually go.

Furthermore, if you can start developing or customizing strategies, do so! Because developing the ability to think and strategize yourself in trade allows you to sift between the lies and mistakes people share with you. The moment you can work matters out for yourself you reduce the risk. So don't be afraid to step in and learn what you can today!

Chapter 9: Understanding Exchanges

Much like you need to use a platform to change money into different currencies, the same can be said for cryptocurrencies. Cryptocurrency exchanges normally facilitate exchanges between different cryptocurrencies as well as fiat currencies. The cryptocurrency exchanges tend to act as the middleman between both the buyer and the seller, and the exchanges to make money via commissions and other fees.

Centralized and Decentralized Exchanges

There are two different types of exchanges, and they have their fair share of differences. The most common and popular form of exchange is the *centralized exchange*, where the exchange official acts as a third party between the buyer and the seller. It is said that about 99% of all exchanges do occur via these platforms, and as a beginner, it is certainly recommended to start this way as well.

There are many advantages that come alongside this form of exchange. For example, the centralized platform is far more user-friendly, offering a familiar as well as a friendly way of trading in comparison to peer-to-peer transactions (decentralized exchanges), which can grow to be quite complex. Simplicity is certainly helpful in any format.

This platform is also far more reliable, adding an extra layer of security when one is actually trading. However, centralized exchanges are at a higher risk of hacking. There were many incidents where hacking has occurred, meaning extra work and effort has to be put in to trust the security of the platform software. Many exchanges hold the value of millions to even potentially billions of dollars worth of money, which makes it a huge digital target.

There are also a lot of transaction fees that come with working on centralized exchanges. The fees will depend on the exchange company you use. You also need to take into account how active you are as a trader, because the costs can add up pretty quickly.

Decentralized exchanges basically allow users to perform peer-to-peer transactions, where you are performing the exchanges directly with the people themselves rather than through a middleman.

When it comes to this platform, there is an automatically reduced risk of hacking, mainly because no one has the need to share third-party information, and because it does not have high-status in popularity, it is much less likely to be a target. These exchanges are automatically far safer in regards to cybercrime.

Market manipulation is a lot more difficult to build in a decentralized system. This is a massive advantage as it gives users a more even playing field. There is a lot of protection from both wash and fake trading.

One of the biggest advantages of crypto is the anonymous nature, so it is no surprise that having a decentralized exchange would play on the advantage of being anonymous as well. Therefore, you can use this platform with the knowledge that you will remain completely anonymous.

However, as mentioned before, decentralized exchanges are a very complex system, which means more time and effort needs to be spent on figuring the exchanges out. This can be very daunting for a beginner, and should only be used if you prefer the advantages of the decentralized system above the centralized system.

Cryptocurrency Exchanges to Consider

Binance

One of the largest cryptocurrency exchanges, in comparison to the trading volume, is Binance. Binance was published by a man named Changpen Zhao in 2017 in China. It has established a reputation of being one of the most reliable exchanges in the crypto trading world. Due to the hurdles faced in China, Binance is now being operated on the Malta islands in Europe. In September 2019, it also launched a platform specifically dedicated for the United States, called Binance US, which is compliant with the regulatory framework of the United States.

Binance is also one of the few exchanges that do not have fake trading volume or even wash trading activities. This means that it is a very transparent and open company. The more transparency that comes with a business, the better.

Binance has also focused on keeping itself up to date with the latest software and technology, making sure to keep up with the competition that is always rapidly advancing. It has managed to establish itself as one of the most popular gateways in the world of crypto.

Binance's History

Binance has attracted a lot of attention due to the cryptocurrency it trades, such as Ethereum and Bitcoin, as well as smaller tokens that are indeed micro-capped. Each token is needed to first fulfill all the requirements, as listed in the Binance rules before being run on this platform.

In 2019, Binance experienced a hack, where the thieves got away with $40 million in Bitcoin. However, the Binance SAFU (Secure Asset Fund Users) Fund had compensated for all the losses, and all the traders who suffered losses were reimbursed. This act certainly boosted Binance's popularity in the entirety of the crypto world.

SAFU is the emergency insurance that was implemented in 2018 as a way to protect trader's funds while they are using the exchange. Having your money insured adds a lot of extra security while you are using the exchange platform, which is especially ideal for a beginner.

Binance's Token

Even Binance has its own native token, called the Binance Coin or BNB, which adds a certain element of competition for its trading fee. The trading fee is reduced when using the platform's token, so fees are even cheaper if you consider using the Binance coin.

Opening a Binance Account

First, you will need to open an account by heading over to the Binance webpage, and you can start off by registering your email address and adding a password. Make sure again that the password you choose is long and complex, as you don't want to be hacked. Again, consider opening up two-factor authentication.

You will need to confirm your own personal details, as a verification of your identity will be required (as expected with a centralized project). This may take a while, as they are very focused on anti-laundering as well as avoiding criminal hubs (which in essence, boosts the security of using the platform, as you would want to make sure you are not dealing with criminals).

Then, after completing the verification process, you can add your funds using either a debit credit or bank accounts, depending on what exactly is supported in your country. Otherwise, you can consider purchasing Bitcoin or Ethereum somewhere else, such as Coinbase, and depositing them onto this platform. When you make the deposit, you can normally start trading within 20 minutes after the deposit has officially been confirmed.

Then you can finally start your journey of trading and investing. You can head to the "Exchange" button that is reflected on the top of the screen, and you can even choose if you want a basic or advanced chart/interface platform you to use. This all depends on what you are more comfortable with, assuming you have undergone paper trading and other training before jumping into live training.

(geralt, 2018)

eToro

eToro is a cheap and professional exchange used by some of the top traders in the world. It is an accessible trading platform that has cleverly devised a social element into investing. They were first launched in early 2006, and are now one of the world's largest communities in investment, with over 4.5 million users.

eToro has a unique feature called the 'copied trader,' where a person can sort through the variety of users and check out their trading history. This is especially handy if you are still learning how to trade and would like to see the choices others have made (do *not* copy-cat). Rather than having to ask the traders, you are free to view the decisions made and whether they were truly successful or not. If you do find someone whose trading choices seem to be doing well, you have the option to allocate funds that can automatically copy the trade. (This means the choices made with funding are in their hands rather than yours, and as the book pushes against it. So you know it is an option, but rather consider studying and learning from them as you build your own path.)

There is another program on eToro called the 'popular investor program.' It acts as a reward system for the number of copiers a specific person has (how many people copy your style and strategy of trading). This boosts the incentive to trade wisely, as people will only copy what they deem to be successful.

With the features tagged on eToro, you can consider this to be a great learning platform, and if you want to familiarize yourself with it without too much of a commitment, you can check it out on a demo account.

Again, before signing up, make sure you understand the basics of trading, and start small. It is never recommended to start investing large amounts of money as a beginner.

Opening an eToro Account

First, you will need to sign up at eToro.com; it is not an extensive application and is quite easy to set up. They do require your phone number in order to boost the security of your account.

It is recommended not to trade using CFD (Contract for Difference Trading) products, as most investors suffer a loss when deciding to do this. So keep this in mind as you start trading.

Next, you will want to fully complete your profile. This is when you input your basic personal information, basically verifying who you are, and have to answer a couple of trading questions. You don't have to be too concerned about the answers, but answer honestly.

Next, you will be directed to the place of deposit, where the minimum amount is normally $200.

Take your time browsing eToro, familiarizing yourself with this platform. You can start by creating a watchlist. This is creating lists of people whose trades you are interested in observing and perhaps considering copying if you want to.

Build your portfolio, which is the center of your journey. Here you can monitor the level of your performance, as well as watch your live trades unfold.

There is also a news feed you can watch, as this is the platform where people keep you updated on what they have been doing recently. This builds a closer community, as many people help each other along with their overall success.

Copy people are the very heart of the community. You can search through many of the traders you want to follow, or if you so, choose to copy.

Robinhood

This is not the legendary archer from the old tales, but rather, this Robinhood is another exchange platform for you to consider. Robinhood has been trending for quite some time, and many experts agree that it is likely to grow in popularity over time. As a crypto investor, you will be more interested in Robinhood Crypto, which acts as the exchange platform for cryptocurrency reviews.

The Robinhood Crypto app truly brought a new item to market in the mobile world. It made the promises for a far easier trading platform (again, ideal for beginners), and garnered the reputation of making trading life a lot simpler for everyone who decides to use it.

Robinhood Crypto supports many of the top cryptocurrencies, which allows you to trade in comfort and ease, and you can deposit or sell crypto to purchase the coins immediately. However, using other items, such as EFT (Electronic Funds Transfer) or stocks, may take up to 3 days to fulfill a trade.

Naturally, there has been a rise in concern about security itself on the crypto app. However, Robinhood did revert to using both online and offline wallets. As already said, offline wallets are far safer, thus boosting the overall security of using Robinhood. The majority of all the coins are kept in cold storage, and the company also carries insurance to make up for cybersecurity attacks and potential breaches.

However, Robinhood Crypto does have its fair share of limitations: one is the inability to withdraw your coins and the other is that you cannot transfer the cryptocurrencies elsewhere in your crypto wallet. However, Robinhood Crypto is working on correcting this limitation and upgrading itself to become more user-friendly.

The Cogworks of Robinhood

If you have a Robinhood account, it means you have instant access to the

Robinhood Crypto account, and even instant access to buying crypto. If you don't, it may take some time to set everything up, including the verification process.

If you have sales from ETFs, it means the money you put in will take a little while longer to arrive, considering you are dealing with the middleman (your bank) and the middleman of the exchange (centralized). This is where patience is needed, but keep in mind you are signing up with Robinhood for its simplicity. If you are struggling to understand the heavy complexities of trading, then perhaps it is best to build your experience on the platform itself.

However, any proceeds that do come from crypto sales are immediately available for your use. And the moment you have the necessary funds, you can focus on buying the coins and start trading as soon as possible.

Selling the coins is as simplified as buying the coins on this app, and all you need to do is navigate the details page, insert the necessary information, and proceed with the sale itself. The moment the coins are sold, you can move on to your next venture with the funds you have received, making this a very effective and efficient trading platform, without the concern of having to wait days or weeks for money to arrive at your door after a trade.

Robinhood itself has taken measures to protect you from the volatile nature of the market, placing a collar on which you can either buy or sell at certain prices that fits within a specific range.

You also have the possibility to use a limit order, programming your account to buy or sell crypto once it reaches a certain price. This is ideal for certain strategies mentioned in the previous chapters and will allow you to stay safe from excessive losses while you are asleep (as it is not possible for you to trade and stay up to date 24/7 unless you intend to go mad). This is a layer of protection, reducing the amount of loss you may receive when the market does not go in a good direction, but also picks up on opportunities that you may miss while you are away. It is an artificial intelligence that does the work of monitoring the trading activities 24/7 while you deal with other priorities.

Robinhood has gained most of its popularity through the design of the app itself. The app is very simple and easy, along with an appealing/aesthetic interface. It also happens to incorporate some of the latest technology, such as a biometric account where you can use your thumbprint to gain access or even your facial ID.

For the purchasing as well as selling of crypto, Robinhood is very easy and simple to use. Literally, with a couple of taps and swipes and clever strategizing (as a savvy investor should), you could easily complete a trade in a matter of minutes. And you can sell it at a rapid pace as well when need be. This certainly makes crypto more interesting for those who struggle to concentrate or figure out the inner workings of a trade. And again, this is quite ideal for a beginner who is still working on figuring everything out when it comes to cryptocurrency trading.

Robinhood also focuses on lower fees in comparison to the 'higher'-level trading sites. To help with people starting out and evening out the playing field, they have removed one of the biggest barriers that comes with trading on exchange platforms: the excessively high trading fees.

This means your sales and trades can work with smaller numbers without the trading fees eating up all your profits, so it is easier to start slow on this platform and still make a profit, regardless of the size of your trade (unless you go lower than the trading fee itself, which is not recommended).

However, there are a few drawbacks that come with trading on this app. One of them that had been mentioned before, is it's functionality. Withdrawal is normally quite an issue, and although you are able to withdraw to your bank account, this does mean incorporating the traditional capital tax that comes alongside it (making the withdrawal of your crypto quite expensive).

There is also a concerning lack of transparency that comes with these prices. Some 'fees' that are supposedly free are just tacked on with the prices people deem the cryptocurrency to be, and this is where Robinhood is actually making the money.

And the team of Robinhood itself has made no comments on the settings of the price of the app, which again, in and of itself can be quite a concerning matter. Transparency is always a big recommendation when it comes to businesses: the less transparency, the more issues the company itself may be trying to hide.

There are also a couple of security concerns, although, unlike some other exchanges, there have been no reports of any large-scale hacks. However, there has been a fair share of cases of isolated hacking occurring in accounts. So the security that is offered on the app is not altogether riskier nor altogether safer than what is being offered on other exchanges. You will have to keep this in mind if safety is a huge priority for you.

So after seeing a little more about Robinhood, you may be wondering whether it is really the right app for you. Each exchange certainly brings something a little different to the table, and it is up to you to decide which exchange suits you the best.

Other Top Exchanges to Consider

Now, having looked in-depth at some of the top exchanges you can consider as a beginner, here is a peek at some of the other top exchanges you can use.

Coinbase

Coinbase and Coinbase Pro have proven to have simplified and easy forms of transactions. The software itself is very transparent, with strong security latched onto it. It is also a very popular form of exchange, and as you work with cryptocurrency and trading you will most likely hear about Coinbase.

Coinbase has a solid variety of altcoins you can trade with. It is also quite user-friendly, and the level of liquidity tacked onto it is high.

But keep in mind, the prices are higher if you are not using Coinbase Pro (trading fees), and a person does not have actual control over their wallet keys. This means that you may need to have another wallet outside of the exchange to store the majority of your coins to make sure they are fully secure.

Coinbase also has a lot of issues with fraudulent coins as well as exchanges that have been quite shady. This means many people avoid these exchanges due to security and higher chances of getting caught in a scam. But Coinbase has offered wallets that are insured for investors as well as insurance for any data breaches that may occur. If you are more advanced, you may consider getting Coinbase Pro, which is more complex, but has a far greater variety of options when it comes to both charts and indicators. This is if you want to trade at a higher level, and would like to have the tools to deal with that.

Cash App

Cash app is another user-friendly exchange app you can use that has quite a few flexible options available, such as the use of other crypto wallets and withdrawals. It is a peer-to-peer money transfer that can work like Venmo or even Zelle. You also have the ability to withdraw Bitcoin itself if you want, and again, being user-friendly makes the life of a trader a lot easier, as there are many fewer frustrations and issues you would have to face.

However, it only actually supports the use of Bitcoin and not any other crypto. There is also a 3% charge when you are sending money through your credit card, and you have a set number of days as well weekly withdrawal limits.

Cash App allows users to invest in other stocks, Bitcoin, or EFTs in a way that Robinhood can as well. It has a simplified mobile interface, making it ideal for people who are investing for the very first time, and beginners who are very much interested in buying Bitcoin.

Having the ability to withdraw your crypto from an exchange is important in the crypto community. With Robinhood, although you can both invest and trade in your cryptocurrencies, you cannot actually withdraw the crypto and spend it in any way you desire. With the Cash App you are fully capable of doing so, but you are actually still unable to gain control of your private keys, which is always a security issue, as you may struggle to prove or gain ownership of the coin if you are not careful.

BiSQ

This is by far one of the best-decentralized forms of exchanges out there. BiSQ is an open-source software that does not have any KYC (Know Your Customer) requirements and is available if you are interested in dabbling in decentralized exchanges in the near future. There are more than 25 varied options you have to pay for, and you can also use it on a mobile app both for Android and also for iOS.

However, the transaction speeds are known to be quite slow, and considering the lack of popularity in using trading volumes, that can be quite slow as well. It is not exactly designed for active forms of trading either.

Following the premise that Bitcoin has set down, there is no requirement for you to legally provide any identification, location, or even nationality on BiSQ. For someone who likes to stay anonymous, this is certainly one of the largest benefits. Considering that many people use crypto for the exact same reason, why not use an exchange that has the same goals?

There are many who argue against the possibility of giving opportunities to criminal activities. There is a flip-side, where people can open accounts that have less-developed banking systems. All you really need is an internet connection. There are millions of people around the world that have minimal access to a bank, which means at the end of the day it inhibits them from trading if they want to. BiSQ very much provides them this opportunity, as it is a good solution for the most part.

It is a downloadable form of software. There is no central point that can fail or be taken down. There is no main point of authority, which means no one ever has any control over the funds of the user, which is vastly different from centralized exchanges. For example, Coinbase, a centralized exchange has every right to seize the funds you have if they deem your activities to be suspicious, regardless of whether what you are doing is actually legal in your specific location.

BISQ is also instantly accessible for anyone who has access to the internet and has a computer or a smartphone. This certainly makes it ideal for anyone who wants to have privacy.

A person has to take into account the lower trading volumes and slower transactions, but for some people, the benefits far outweigh the drawbacks. And again, it is up to you to decide.

When you are looking for a cryptocurrency trading or investing platform, it is best to choose the exchange that suits your goals. Whether it may be cheaper fees, easier design, or even a variety of coins, these are all matters you will have to consider when approaching the exchange. So it is best to have your goals in place first before deciding on the exchange, rather than adapting to the exchange. After all, this is your journey, and you best make sure you are actually comfortable with the steps you are taking.

Conclusion

There is no doubt about the fact that you have a lot more to learn about cryptocurrency, but as you can see here, it is not so difficult after all. Just dense. Cryptocurrency has a lot that you need to know, a lot you need to take into consideration, and a lot of factors that you will have to decide for yourself. A few years ago, there weren't many choices you could make, but with an ever-growing, advancing world, there are more choices than you can even comprehend. Information is your greatest ally, and the best part? Most of it is freely available for you. All you need to learn is to filter truth from fib, and work your way from there.

Although it is good to listen to the advice of others, it is best to adapt your choices to suit your circumstances (a factor many people tend to forget when pushing you to make a decision). When it comes to cryptocurrency, you have to take responsibility for your decisions, because despite having followed someone else's bad advice, it is ultimately you that lost the money. So isn't it best to have no one but yourself to blame if losses are incurred by a mistake you made? It is far worse to have fallen for a scam, or blindly followed a tip that ultimately caused your failure, especially if you would have chosen differently, had you decided to be in control.

Furthermore, cryptocurrency is volatile by nature. Everywhere you go and look, this factor pops up. So much so, it would be foolish to ignore it (although too many people still do). And so, it is best to invest only money you can actually afford to lose. In fact, it is best that cryptocurrency does not make up the entirety of your investments, but just a small part. Apart from its potentially high returns, you have a greater chance for higher losses. If those losses do occur, you may not feel it as much if you have invested in other options as well. Again, how you diversify your portfolio is all up to you. It is officially in your hands, and who knows where this pathway will take you.

When starting off as well, remember to take it slowly. Diving into the deep end of the pool will do no one any favors as the risk of loss can certainly outweigh the learning process that comes with it. Don't consider letting yourself into the deep end this time, with cryptocurrency, you are far more likely to drown than with a different investment.

Finally, learn to have fun with it. Taking on cryptocurrency out of a need or pure desire to earn will bring nothing but stress and problems. Rather, find ways to enjoy it, setting up achievable goals, and making bets with yourself. Challenge yourself to learn as much as you can about crypto, and take losses with the mindset of learning. Don't give in to defeat or panic.

Remember that research and patience are your two greatest allies when it comes to the world of cryptocurrency. Avoid hurdles, such as peer pressure, common scams, and poor investment choices. Having both the dedication and patience to do research is one of the primary characteristics of a savvy trader.

Now you have the foundational knowledge of crypto, as well as the key steps to start your trading journey, don't hesitate to start today, whether by paper simulations or small trades that you can afford to lose if the worst occurs. Remember, the harder you work, the better your chances of success. Practice makes perfect after all. And the scariest reality is the factor that just putting a little extra effort already gets you the edge over most other investors, who tend to walk into these things blindly.

However, please do keep in mind that this book is designed for educational purposes, and not meant to be professional/financial recommendations. That means that although the information is intended to help your trading journey, it is not guaranteed to help you succeed.

Still, everything given here is meant to help you grow. Cryptocurrency is no easy feat, but many people want to take part in it because it is growing in prominence and importance. There are still many factors holding people back, such as its volatile nature. But if you are willing to take on the risk, then you will be participating in the rise of a new digital era.

References

common stock investing mistakes to avoid as a beginner. (2020, April 25). Groww. https://groww.in/blog/common-stock-investing-mistakes-to-avoid-as-a-beginner/

ways to prepare for a market crash. (2021). Investopedia. https://www.investopedia.com/articles/financial-advisors/100615/how-protect-your-portfolio-market-crash.asp

trading strategies every trader should know. (2021). CMC markets. https://www.cmcmarkets.com/en/trading-guides/trading-strategies

common investment scams (2018, December 13). GetSmarterAboutMoney.ca. https://www.getsmarteraboutmoney.ca/protect-your-money/fraud/protecting-against-fraud/8-common-investment-scams/

breakdown on how the stock market works. (2021). Investopedia. https://www.investopedia.com/articles/investing/082614/how-stock-market-works.asp

ustralian Competition and Consumer Commission. (2015, June 23). *Protect yourself from scams.* Australian Competition and Consumer Commission. https://www.scamwatch.gov.au/get-help/protect-yourself-from-scams

void these 8 common investing mistakes. (2021). Investopedia. https://www.investopedia.com/articles/stocks/07/beat_the_mistakes.asp

est crypto exchanges. (2021). Investopedia. https://www.investopedia.com/best-crypto-exchanges-5071855

inance review 2021: Pros, cons, fees, features, and safety. (2021, February 24). InsideBitcoins. ttps://insideBitcoins.com/cryptocurrency-exchanges/binance-review

reaking down Stellar coin's pros and cons. (2021, January 15). Nasdaq.com. https://www.nasdaq.com/articles/breaking-down-stellar-coins-pros-and-cons-2021-01-15

orporate Finance Institute. (2020, December 21). *Cryptocurrency exchanges.* Corporate Finance Institute. https://corporatefinanceinstitute.com/resources/knowledge/other/cryptoc

exchanges/

Davis, C. (2017, February 3). *How to buy stocks.* NerdWallet. https://www.nerdwallet.com/article/investing/how-to-buy-stocks

Elearnmarkets. (2019, June). *25 stock market terms a beginner should know.* Elearnmarkets. https://www.elearnmarkets.com/blog/stock-market-terms-a-beginner-should-know/#:~:text=Buy%20%E2%80%93%20Means%20to%20buys%20sh

Toro: The world's leading social trading and investing platform. (2020). Etoro.com. https://www.etoro.com/?dl=30001923&utm_medium=Affiliate&utm_source=49106&utm_conte

Fankhauser, D. (2021, June 22). *Robinhood Crypto review: The pros, cons and how it compares.* Bitcompare. https://bitcompare.net/reviews/robinhood

Tran, B. (2021, June 24). 6 tips to exchange currency without paying huge fees. *Forbes.* https://www.forbes.com/advisor/banking/exchange-currency-without-paying-huge-fees/

How to buy and sell stocks on your own. (2021). Investopedia. https://www.investopedia.com/ask/answers/108.asp

How to invest in the stock market using eToro. (2015, February 11). Save the Student. https://www.savethestudent.org/make-money/stock-market-investing.html

How to pick a stock: Basic best practices for new investors. (2021). Investopedia. https://www.investopedia.com/articles/basics/11/how-to-pick-a-stock.asp

I want to start buying stocks—But where do I start? (2021). Investopedia. https://www.investopedia.com/ask/answers/05/042205.asp

Inflation. (2021). Investopedia. https://www.investopedia.com/terms/i/inflation.asp

Investopedia stock simulator. (2021). Investopedia. https://www.investopedia.com/simulator/

Kaspersky. (2021, January 13). *4 common cryptocurrency scams and how to avoid them.* https://www.kaspersky.com/resource-center/definitions/cryptocurrency-scams

Kulkarni, S. (2021, May 17). *Bitcoin: Pros and cons of investing in world's largest cryptocurrency.* Goodreturns. https://www.goodreturns.in/classroom/pros-and-cons-of-investing-in-Bitcoin-advantages-and-disadvantages-of-Bitcoin-cryptocurrency-

1209500.html

Liebkind, J. (2020, September 24). *Beware of these five Bitcoin scams.* Investopedia. https://www.investopedia.com/articles/forex/042315/beware-these-five-bitcoin-scams.asp

Naranjian, S. (2019, March 20). *20 common beginner investor mistakes, and how to avoid them.* The Motley Fool; The Motley Fool. https://www.fool.com/retirement/beginner-investor-mistakes-how-to-avoid.aspx

Miller, P. (2021, July 18). *Common cryptocurrency scams to look out for.* The Daily Californian. https://www.dailycal.org/2021/07/17/common-cryptocurrency-scams-to-look-out-for/

Neo blockchain platform cons, pros & what's NEO's dBFT algorithm? (2019, September 18). Science Online. https://www.online-sciences.com/cryptocurrency/neo-blockchain-platform-cons-pros-whats-neos-dbft-algorithm/

Robinhood Crypto. (2021). Robinhood. https://robinhood.com/us/en/about/crypto/

Schaefer, S. (2016, June 20). 10 things you absolutely need to know about stocks. *Forbes.* https://www.forbes.com/sites/steveschaefer/2016/01/05/10-things-you-absolutely-need-to-know-about-stocks/?sh=6ef3baeb3f57

SoFi. (2021, January 8). *A brief history of the stock market.* SoFi. https://www.sofi.com/learn/content/history-of-the-stock-market/?__cf_chl_jschl_tk__=52d0835ec51e1384d18215391cd2209e74dbe4d4-1623436056-0-ATVAJKQM4KvCf0t1eeK2lrPcwW7Cqo7jdxXObp8wzV-x1CjjEHmSnFT0vwUylZovEkeqmRuA-3M8LWIOAnRPQWpM6GycJuU82uW-W4U3s1Rc-fpYHmZGPYWJSCDtJOrwPfVTEnCG0WTOf8sHQ4g5wFvcoVCV163AkFXSiVnkb0pD14fzRDAqVc_d_A1lIBB-CeUE7jdif-POu4UcZfaho4fsvoRpP-7hAfa2LGMNpR-jPRcG-lDULBxnijw1JVFzbq-JdASlnxi3kRV9nuTQrGtSoCj2-OEVZ-YSuMGNff5hbamVe7k_nORhMvAKXPu1h_IXjs0GiC7dAvXT-sU9ksmZYLZ-6DQbzobrbGEdv_7aeiw1O0cN4AyDFdfgzK00GgA-iuuCn778ZJRcE3wXby-_jg tammers, R. (n.d.). *Tips for avoiding the top 20 common investment mistakes.* Retrieved August 5, 2021, https://www.cfainstitute.org/-/media/documents/support/future-finance/avoiding-common-investor-mistakes.ashx

tock market. (2021). Investopedia. https://www.investopedia.com/terms/s/stockmarket.asp

he stop-loss order—Make sure you use it. (2021). Investopedia. https://www.investopedia.com/articles/stocks/09/use-stop-loss.asp

op 10 rules for successful trading. (2021). Investopedia. https://www.investopedia.com/articles/trading/10/top-ten-rules-for-trading.asp

rading Education Team. (2020, November 12). *Pros and cons of investing in Ethereum: Will it be a millionaire maker?* Trading Education. https://trading-education.com/pros-and-cons-of-investing-in-Ethereum-will-it-be-a-millionaire-maker

rading Education Team. (2020, December 3). *Pros and cons of investing in Litecoin: Will it be a millionaire maker?* Trading Education. https://trading-education.com/pros-and-cons-of-investing-in-Litecoin-will-it-be-a-millionaire-maker

rading Education Team. (2021, January 19). *Pros and cons of investing in Cardano: Will it be a millionaire maker?* Trading Education. https://trading-education.com/pros-and-cons-of-investing-in-cardano

*oigt, K. (2018, July 16). *5 stock market strategies for beginners.* NerdWallet. https://www.nerdwallet.com/article/investing/stock-market-strategies-for-beginners

*oigt, K. (2020, February). *eToro review 2021: Pros, cons and how it compares.* NerdWallet. https://www.nerdwallet.com/reviews/investing/brokers/etoro

*ulcan Post. (2021, March 14). *The pros and cons for Ethereum investors.* Vulcan Post. https://vulcanpost.com/738641/the-pros-and-cons-for-Ethereum-investors/

hy NEO can do what no other cryptocurrency can do. (2021). Investopedia. https://www.investopedia.com/tech/china-neo-cryptocurrency/

ll images sourced from Pixabay.com.

www.ingramcontent.com/pod-product-compliance
Lightning Source LLC
Chambersburg PA
CBHW081823200326

41597CB00023B/4370